TSOG

TSOG:

The Thing That Ate The Constitution

and other everyday monsters

Robert Anton Wilson

NEW FALCON PUBLICATIONS
TEMPE, ARIZONA, U.S.A.

International Standard Book Number: 1-56184-169-2
Library of Congress Catalog Card Number: 2002105417

First Edition 2002

Cover and illustrations by Linda Joyce Franks
Photograph of Robert Anton Wilson by Lance Bauscher

The paper used in this publication meets the minimum requirements of the American National Standard for Permanence of Paper for Printed Library Materials Z39.48-1984.

Address all inquiries to:
NEW FALCON PUBLICATIONS
1739 East Broadway Road #1-277
Tempe, AZ 85282 U.S.A.
(or)
320 East Charleston Blvd. #204-286
Las Vegas, NV 89104 U.S.A.
website: http://www.newfalcon.com
email: info@newfalcon.com

to
Paul Krassner,
Zen Bastard

Contents

The New World Order

Contract

1. The author of this book hereby warrants and gives assurance that the readers have no obligation to believe everything—or anything—in it. Nor does he hope to reveal the absolute & final truth about any topic discussed.

2. Readers must warrant and gives assurance that they will not believe or disbelieve any part or parts of this book until they have given some time to careful examination of such a part or parts; and that they will file everything herein under "maybe" until or unless slowly arriving at "true" or "false."

3. Let communication between us begin.

_____
Signature of reader

Robert Anton Wilson
_____
Signature of author

Another golden passage occurs in *Politics* (1310a9) where Aristotle states plainly that in the first nations the rich swore themselves to eternal hatred of the common people. This self-evident truth explains the pride, avarice and cruelty of the rich... They compelled the poor to serve them in war...drowned them in an ocean of usury...and beat them with rods if they could not pay their debts.

— Giambattista Vico, *The New Science,* 1744

The Old World

When you no longer think of good or evil, What is your original face? If you turn your light towards the interior, you will discover the precious secret within yourself.

— Hui Neng

TEMPORARY AUTONOMOUS ZONE

I felt as cold as Paddy Finnegan's feet the day they hanged him. I could sense my legs *physically* shivering, a strange sensation for somebody who lives in central California. The shivering turned to trembling: I wondered if anybody passing thought I was epileptic.

We were standing, a small crew of us, on one of those concrete islands between two traffic lanes outside the Amsterdam airport, and the icy wind seemed as relentless as an unpaid Madam. We stood in a wide-open space with no tall buildings and we might as well have been sailing on the North Sea. I wanted to creep home to sunny California. I wanted to drop out of the goddam 12th Annual Cannabis Cup and go someplace, anyplace, that was not northern Europe in the winter. I was 68 years old and felt like I'd been shivering for 67 of them.

I wondered how the others could remain so cheerful, and felt ashamed of my weakness.

I went on shivering and feeling guilty about it.

After an hour, the Cannabis Cup bus arrived and I was delivered to the American Hotel, where those lovely folks from *High Times* did everything they could to make me comfortable and get me bombed and generally compensate me for my chilling experience at the airport. After the first joint, I still felt as frozen solid as the iceberg that sank the Titanic, so they gave me a second joint. Since the American is well-heated, and cannabis, after all, is cannabis, in a short while I couldn't remember turning into Frosty the Snowman at the airport or anything else to be grumpy about.

I migrated to the bar with Anthony Countey of *High Times* and we discussed the Cannabis Cup over Jameson's whiskey and coffee. I pointed out that everybody at the Cup understood the synergetic advantage of mixing cannabis and caffeine but only I

17

knew the Mystery of the Holy Trinity—pot, caffeine and Jameson's—which I had discovered while living in Ireland. "Let the squares have their Valium and other tranks," I said, "I've found God's Own Cure-All."

When jet lag set in and I retired to my room, I looked over the City Guide and noted with some interest that the Red Light District was clearly marked as a tourist attraction. O Amsterdam..."the best window-shopping in Europe"...

Curious, I started looking for the cannabis coffee houses and couldn't find any. Evidently the American Hotel assumes that their male guests will all want a Personalized First Class Grade A Amsterdam-Style Blow Job but aren't interested in getting stoned. I decided they were mistaken: to fully appreciate a first-class Blow Job, even Amsterdam-Style, requires a bit of Dat Debbil Weed before you even go to the Ho House, suh.

Tiredly, I wondered why "Dutch" has so many negative con-notations in American speech. The "Dutch Act" means suicide. "Dutch Courage" means booze. To get "in dutch" in my youth meant "getting inna shit," as we say today. A "Dutch uncle" is harsh and judgmental. At a "Dutch treat" you pay for yourself. Ben Jonson killed a Spaniard in Holland. Then I "heard" in imagination the overture to Wagner's *Der Fliegende Hollander*, and then I was dozing in my chair, still zonked, and dreaming of Flying Dutchmen and then Flying Scandinavians in general, including my ancestor, Olaf the Black, who was once King of the Isle of Man, which has crossed keys on its flag, and I turned the keys and crossed to the House of Keyes in the unmarked state. Then I seemed inside no spatial time.

Then my wife Arlen and I were dancing—dancing together again—and Thelonious Monk music from our youth was playing and she wasn't dead and I wasn't old and the world was full of magic and wonder. ***Ubi amor, ibi oculus est.***

—————

Save the Earth!
It's the only planet with chocolate.

—————

Then it was the third day of the Cannabis Cup and four of us were sitting in a coffee house called Noon and smoking something called "Purple Purple." "Uh…" Anthony Countey said to the waitcritter (a word I use in order to avoid the human chauvinism of "waitperson") "Uh…have we paid yet?"

The waitcritter looked at us with the painstaking concentration of a botanist examining a strange new carnivorous specimen. "Uh…," she said, "Uh… I *think* so."

I suddenly remembered a local TV host, who had interviewed me the day before. He had mentioned in passing that 360 coffee shops in Amsterdam sold cannabis with their coffee and that they earned about US$1,000,000 per year *each*. I had multiplied it in my head and emerged with the figure of $360,000,000 per year in profits. That's over a billion every three years. Now I wondered how much higher the profits might be if the management could persuade the staff not to sample the product.

Anthony and the waitcritter continued to stare at each other with perplexity, like two chessmasters wondering how they had wandered into the Ourang Outan Opening.

"Uh," she said finally, "If you didn't pay, it's on the house."

We had to rush off to attend another scheduled event, but all across Amsterdam in the taxi I kept trying to remember if we had paid or not, and, if not, how much that really mattered in the Cosmic Scheme of Things. But I always mull about the Cosmic Scheme when I've been stoned every hour for three days. I was distracted from such Deep Thoughts for a moment by idle curiosity about where the last three days had gone.

The Noon coffee shop, Anthony had told me, was originally called the High Noon. But somebody in the city government forced them to drop the "High": you can sell pot in Amsterdam, he explained, but you can't be *blatant* about it. I remembered my first visit to Amsterdam in the early 1980's, when every bridge, it seemed, had an ad for one of those establishments; when I returned about two years later the ads had all disappeared but the coffee houses hadn't, and they were still serving cannabis with their caffeine.

The Dutch... Go figure.

I once met a gingkus who believed that Dutch bankers own controlling shares in the major English and American banks, who in turn own the English and American governments, who run most of the world. I pondered this variation 5E/23a on the International Bankers Conspiracy. I pondered it deeply, and I found myself wondering why these crafty old Dutchman had never persuaded the Ango-American cabal to adapt their own pragmatic attitude toward Sex'n'Drugs. Maybe they wanted to keep a monopoly on the legal end of the Hedonism business? A billion every three years seems tempting; why encourage the eejit puritans to accept Adam Smith's free market and maybe start competing?

But what had happened to the last three days?

Suddenly a **red-white-and-blue** brontosaurus reared up in front of us. The taxi driver steered around it and I watched in awe as it turned into to a VW bus. I made a mental note of the name of Noon and "Purple Purple" for the next time I visit Amsterdam. After all, I haven't seen a red-white-and-blue dinosaur since the first time I did raw peyote in 1962.

The day before (or was it the day before that?) came back in another flash. The TV guy, after interviewing me, had taken me to the Sea Palace, a superb Chinese restaurant on a houseboat with glorious views, which I remembered from a few years ago. His wife-or-girl-friend (you don't ask nowadays) kept trying to persuade me that Scientific Research was responsible for all the ills of the world. "You don't need research," she said, "your heart tells you the truth." The Inquisitors had tried to tell that to Galileo.

The TV guy told me some statistics which I copied down. There were about 2000 people at the Cup this year, 1400 of them from the United States. I had heard that there were fewer than 100 at the first Cup, twelve years ago, and I mulled on the Miracle of Growth.

"Torturing helpless animals," the lady said. "Research! Phooey!"

Without censorship, things can get terribly confused in the public mind.

— General William Westmoreland

The next day, after some spooky but mellow weed called Silver Haze, I went to the Van Gogh Museum. As usual, Vincent seemed the greatest artist in the history of the world, to me at least. I think he got me even Higher than the Silver Haze.

I jotted a note: "Cure for depression—

1. Go to Amsterdam.
2. Get stoned.
3. Go to Van Gogh Museum."

I even thought of sending this "discovery" in a letter to a medical magazine. Well, you get foolishly optimistic on cannabis and Van Gogh.

Coming back to the Cup, I passed the famous sex-theatre, which still has an enormous billboard, bigger than any in Times Square, saying:

LIVE
FUCKING
INSIDE

You gotta love a town like that.

Just after that, or just before it, I was at a Cannabis Cup event where Steve Hager gave a speech saying pot-heads had replaced Jews as the Number One International Government-Designated Scapegoats. We were smoking some more loverly Silver Haze. I speculated that the 1400 Americans had come here, not just for the congenial company, but to get high without having to worry that the TSOGestapo might smash down the door at any moment. *Under Clinton, we now have more people in prison than any other country in the world,* and they're building more prisons every day. We even have a Tsar, although no such office is mentioned in the Constitution.

After the position was created, I looked up "Tsar" in my dictionary. The first two meanings did not seem to apply: "1. The ruler of Russia"; "2. Eldest male member of the Romanoff family"; but the third hit the nail square on the head: "3. Any tyrant or autocrat."

I was sitting at a table with Paul Krassner, whom I had known for 40 years and 5 months. I couldn't calculate to the day because I did not quite remember what day it was. But I know I got the years and months right because I met Paul the day my son, Graham, was born, 5 June 1959.

Paul asked when I first smoked pot. I wasn't sure whether it was 1955 or 1956, but I said 1955, because I like to think of myself as a pioneer. Whatever the year, that Historical Event happened in the Men's Room at the Village Vanguard between sets by the Modern Jazz Quartet. John Lewis sounded better than ever when the show resumed—but you know that already.

Paul asked John Sinclair, also at our table, when he had Turned On. Since John's hair was as white as mine, I wondered if he might beat me out in the pioneer competition, but he said 1963. Paul then asked Steve Gaskin when he smoked his first joint, and Steve said 1962.

I basked in my glory as oldest pioneer at the table, meanwhile wondering how my four decades on pot have fucked up mah pore ole haid. In that whole time I only produced 11 novels, 2 screenplays, one stage play, 20 nonfiction books and a few thousand short articles and poems. Could I have done better without the Hoodoo Weed? I puzzled over that, meanwhile puzzling over the ineluctable fact that John Sinclair didn't look at all like I remembered him. We all change with the years, and white hair and a white beard add to that, but this metamorphoses seemed almost like a Hollywood special effect. I worried that the stuff we were then smoking, Midnight Sunrise, might have interacted with the Purple Purple and Silver Haze and John might turn into a Purple Purple Hippopotamus next.

Steve Gaskin—founder of The Farm, one of the damned few New Age communes which have lasted from the 1960's to today— told us he was running against Ralph Nader for the Green Party presidential nomination. His platform includes free medical care for all, legalization of pot, and compulsory urine testing for government employees to make sure they maintain a high enough THC level.

I decided to heckle him a little, because he had persuaded me to vote for Clinton-Gore back in 1992, telling me Gore was a long-time pot-head. "You still trust those Lying Bastards?" I asked.

Steve said, "They fooled me." He said it so gently and softly that I had no inclination to pester him about that anymore. Hell, they fooled me, too.

Steve's wife, Ina May, president of the Midwives Association of North America, said that she would be "an unruly First Lady." She plans to turn the Lincoln Bedroom into a birth center for the poor, grow hemp in the Rose Garden, and make all meals at the White House vegetarian. Somebody asked if she has intern concerns, and she replied, "No, we'll do the Blow Jobs in every room."

I liked all that, as long as I don't have to eat at the White House, but what I liked best was Steve's running against Ralph

Nader. Every time I have to attach a seat-belt I say "God *damn* Ralph Nader," with the fervid intensity of a child's prayer, even though I don't believe in God or damnation; it relieves my feelings. I mean, just because Nader is a bondage freak doesn't give him the right to truss us all up. The next thing we know the creep will get a law passed compelling me to be strapped to my chair while writing so I don't laugh so hard that I fall over and hurt myself.

I told Ina May how much my wife Arlen had admired her and the midwifery movement in general. I added that I agreed, but didn't explain that this was based on my belief that the best way to stay healthy is to avoid doctors as much as possible.

John Sinclair began talking about his days with the MC-5, a great Rock group of the 1960's. My brain did a quantum jump and reorganized the whole world. This was not the John Sinclair I once knew, who wrote a brilliant column for the *Village Voice*. No wonder he didn't look like "himself": he wasn't "himself" at all. He was the *other* John Sinclair, from Detroit, who founded the White Panther Party and served a few years in prison for generously giving a joint to an undercover narc. (Under Michigan law at that time, giving somebody a good high for free was punished with the same imprisonment as selling it.) I had just mixed up two different John Sinclairs.

I felt relieved. Mixing all that fucking pot hadn't fucked up my fucking brain after all.

They led me to the stage. (Was it the same day or another day?) I was giving a speech, inducting William S. Burroughs into the Cannabis Hall of Fame. I told them all the reasons I consider Burroughs the greatest writer since Joyce, but they seemed restless, so I quoted them a bit of unpublished Burroughs:

> A coprophile named Scott
> Who lived in Aldershott
> Said, "I'm unbeatable—
> My shit is eatable!
> Perpetual motion I've got."

I went into flashback...... November 1968, at the Playboy Club in Chicago, having lunch with Burroughs and Allen Ginsberg. We had been Demonstrating Against The War all week, but now we were enjoying a pleasant meal, and Allen was telling us about his recent meeting with Crazy Uncle Ezra in Rapollo. He had told Ez he considered the *Cantos* the greatest poem of the 20th Century, and Ez said, "But it is all vitiated by that stupid, suburban anti-semitism."

"*Suburban*," Burroughs repeated, considering the connotations of the word; I was more fascinated by "vitiated."

I snapped back to Amsterdam. We were all going to an American-style Thanksgiving dinner. But we had some more Silver Haze first. It was a long walk and three flights of stairs to climb before we got at the grub. My legs hurt and all the white meat was gone but I took some dark with assorted vegetables and found a table with Carolyn and John Cassidy, the widow and son of the fabled Neal Cassidy. I recited my usual grace, "Damn all this self-improvement, I want a pleasant dinner," which I have borrowed from Hannibal Lecter, M.D.

While we ate and chatted, I kept peeking at John Cassidy's hair. Was he just an exceptionally light blonde, or did he have some white hair, too? Could Neal Cassidy's son really have white hair already? Where have all the past years gone, "and where are the snows of yesteryear?/Where is Joan, that the English took/At Rouenville and burned her there?/Mother of God, where are they, where?/And where are the snows of yesteryear?" I suddenly felt as old as the Mohave Desert and wondered if I looked like a dead mule.

The next day they announced the winner of the Cannabis Cup—the best brand of Maria Juana in Amsterdam. Silver Haze had won, and I guess it should have.

As I flew home I realized that Amsterdam had once again renewed my optimism: civilization *remains* possible, even on this backward boondocks planet. You just have to look awfully hard to find it. Back in the U.S., among those whom Veblen accurately called the Higher Barbarians, it is good to recall such an autonomous zone: memories of it stave off total despair.

PARADISE LOST

A few months later, back in California, I got out of bed one morning and fell down three times on my way to the bathroom. After the third and hardest bump I stayed on the carpet a while, wondering anxiously if I had just had a stroke. Arlen had her first stroke right after getting out of bed one morning. My turn now?

Tentatively, an inch at a time, I got to my feet again and stood; then I went to the john and peed.

Not a stroke, I decided. But I almost fell a fourth time on my way to the kitchen to start the coffee.

My legs had hurt more than usual in the last month. My doctor had warned me that post-polio symptoms get worse as you get older...

I sat with the coffee, looking at my splendid view of Monterey Bay, and pondered.

Then I called the doctor.

———

It isn't pollution that's harming the environment. It's the impurities in our air and water that are doing it.
— Former U. S. Vice-president Dan Quayle

———

One year later...

After a year spent mostly in a wheelchair, I now get around with the aid of a walker most of the time, and only need the wheelchair occasionally. I continue to improve—not as quickly as I would like, but then I tend to be an impatient bastard.

Pain has decreased about 70%, partly due to pain-killers, possibly to healing and recuperation also.

Mobility increases more slowly. I can manage 10 or 15 paces without my walker, but beyond that pain and wobble (unsteadiness) warn me to stop. Last Monday, in a fit of optimism, I walked about 40 paces without the walker, and my left leg hurt for about two hours after, even with pain-killers. Well, that's profitable, too: I have finally learned the virtue of patience.

Meanwhile, I have researched this predicament a bit.

Number of U.S. polio survivors appears between 300,000 and 1,600,000, depending on which website I consult. Number with PPS is between 75,000 and 1,200,000, according to various websites. PPS means either post-polio *syndrome* or post-polio *sequelae*. The prognosis is either terrible or hopeful.

None of this confusion surprises me. According to a study by the Office of Technology Assessment only 20% of American medical theory has been validated by randomized, double-blind, placebo-controlled trials. About 80% of the time, then, doctors follow prejudice, hunch, intuition, guessing, prayer, or just plain bluff. (See my *Chaos and Beyond*, p. 31.)

Times of onset of PPS vary from 10 years after polio to 50 years after. (Mine began, mildly, 20 years after, got worse slowly beginning 40 years after, and hit hardest 64 years after—i.e., at age 68.)

———•◆•———

"Post-polio syndrome" is the term preferred by those who believe the condition is fundamentally incurable and generally worsens with age. "Post-polio sequelae" is preferred by those who think the problem can be much improved and stabilized.

The **PPSyn** Experts believe the symptoms result from surviving polio virus which suddenly begins multiplying like Catholics again. The **PPSeq** Experts believe the symptoms result from decades of stress and strain on muscles that were damaged during the polio. Both sides seem to want a good old-fashioned aristotelian either/or battle over this. However, unlike the similar feud

about AIDS, neither side has urged the jailing of the other—
probably because there's less money involved.

Having a non-aristotelian bias, I consider the Excluded Middles; e.g., some PPS cases result from surviving virus and some
from overstressed muscles; some combine both; some have only a
coincidental link to past polio and result from Other Factors, e.g.,
living near a toxic waste dump, poor diet over decades, etc.; some
may result from depletion of the immunological system due to
shock or grief; some may combine several of these aspects.

My own case—I feel about 90% sure—results mostly from
stressed muscles. I have 1001 experiential reasons for "believing"
this, or at least considering it the highest probability. Chief reason:
pain experienced all my adult life while standing on lines—at
banks, supermarkets, etc., but especially on the long, long lines at
airports. Sometimes, beginning in my late 50s, the pain at airports
has gotten so intense that I have felt tempted to explain the problem and ask to go to the front of the line. I never actually tried it
because I never looked "disabled" and feared everybody would
suspect me of running a con on them. I stood and shuffled and
suffered.

Just as I stood and shuffled and suffered in the cold at Amsterdam airport. PPS makes you feel 20 degrees colder than people
without PPS; I just hadn't known that at the time. I had felt
ashamed of suffering more than the others.

Until the PPSyn experts explain why my alleged virus only
erupted when I stood on a long lines and then "died" again when I
get a chance to sit down, I will prefer the PPSeq theory of damaged
muscles under six decades of overwork from trying to act like
normal muscles.

My current therapy involves precursors of Human Growth
Hormone, to rebuild the stressed, cramped muscles; mild exercize—*mild* so as not to stress the muscles even more; and lying
down to rest when I feel I need it. My pain-killers are ibuprofen—
recommended by my daughter, Chistina, six years ago—and
cannabis, recommended (but not, God forfend, "prescribed") by
my physician, and provided by the Women's Alliance for Medical
Marijuana. In tincture form, the Weed kills pain very, very quickly

(quarter hour average, often less) but also tends to knock me out and force frequent naps and less work. It doesn't get me high at all, at all. In muffin form, the Weed does get me high—often hilariously—and allows (nay, **ENCOURAGES**) me to go on working, but takes much longer to kill pain (one to two hours).

We will now pause for a chorus of "We need more research/ Meanwhile, let the victims suffer" by the Two Lying Bastards, the popular clown show featuring Gore and Bore, or Bush and Bushwah, as the case may be.

I no longer fear the TSOG (Tsarist Occupation Government). If they throw my arse in jail, well, there's more pot inside than outside; and *convicts & Congress, our two criminal classes, are the only ones who have full medical coverage.* Outside those institutions for known felons, one has only one's earning capacity to fill the bottomless pit of AMA greed, and I have to face the possibility that my condition may not continue to improve but worsen, thereby decreasing income. Since I obviously can't get into Congress—I never learned to lie with a straight face—prison may prove the best alternative.

PS—Bore and Gush can go bugger themselves. Or one another, if they prefer.

**the
Farben
works
still
intact**

The New World

And against usury
    and the degradation of sacraments,
For 40 years I have seen this,
    now flood as in the Yang-tse
also desensitization
    25 hundred years desensitization
    2 thousand years, desensitization
After Appolonius, desensitization
    & a little light from the borders
        — Ezra Pound, Canto 92

TSOG:
THE THING THAT ATE THE CONSTITUTION

Tsarism represents an intermediate form between European monarchism and Asian despotism, being, possibly, closer to the latter of these two.

> — Leon Trotsky,
> *Russia's Social Development and Tsarism*

The TSOG stalketh the land and the serfs bow and worship it. It stealeth property, it burneth neighborhoods, it foully killeth all opposition. Ye think it only doth its violence to black people, or Hispanics, or kooks with odd religions, but its hand is at your own throat even now. *TSOG fthagn!* What—are ye stupid, or something?

> — Abdul Alhazred, *The TSOGonomicon*

I'm only kidding—not!

> — Madonna, *Truth or Dare*

How, how, how did we ever get ourselves in a predicament where an Oriental-style despot controls American medicine and most doctors fear to prescribe what they think best for their patients? Why, more than 200 years after a war to liberate ourselves from a half-mad king, have we allowed our lives and health to come under the rule of a totally mad Tsar? And has this monstrous tumor destroyed the Constitution only "by accident," or did its creators have that intent all along?

Well, here's my theory:

Most people think the TSOG (Tsarist Occupation Government) began its infestation of America with Bushware 1.0, when he appointed a Tsar to discombobulate our previously "demO-kratic form of gubment;" but Bush had a long C.I.A. career behind him and the C.I.A. had a long, long Tsarist history before they came out in the open with a public and blatant Tsar—a functionary not endowed or permitted by any clause in our Constitution.

Actually, the TSOG began replacing representative democracy in the U.S. way back in 1945, when Gen. Rheinhard Gehlen, Hitler's Chief of Soviet Intelligence, surrendered to the U.S. Army after first prudently burying several truckloads of "inside information" about the Soviet Union at a secret location. (The Cold War began before World War II ended; they just didn't bother to tell the serfs like you and me about it until 1947.)

Gehlen ranks as not only a master spy but a wizard negotiator. Within a week, he got out of his Nazi uniform and into a U.S. Army General's uniform; the U.S. intelligence services, in return, got the info about the Soviets, including access to Gehlen's agents in the Soviet government—a group of Mystical Tsarists who had infiltrated both the Red Army and the KGB.

You see, their leader and Gehlen's major "asset," General Andrei Vlassov, had a fervent belief, not just in common or garden-variety Tsarism, but especially in the "mystical Tsarism" espoused in the latter half of the 19th Century by the anti-Semitic novelist Dostoyevsky and even more by Konstantin Pobedonostsev, an advisor to two Tsars (Alexander III and Nicholas II).

Pobedonostsev, popularly called "The Grand Inquisitor" because of the vast platoons of spies, snoops, *agents provocateur* and informers he unleashed upon the Russian people, combined theological obsessions with reactionary politics, always an explosive and nefarious mixture.

"Mystical Tsarism," a holy religion, or crazy superstition—as you will—has two major tenets: (1) The Tsar is guided by God and can do no wrong, and (2) Reason is "cold" and inhuman, faith is "warm" and human; therefore we should ignore reason and guide ourselves by faith in the Tsar, our "Little Father." I don't think any of Pobedonostsev's crew actually believed in the Tooth Fairy, though.

Besides, Roman Catholics of the old school have similar attitudes, but merely prefer a Pope to do their thinking for them instead of a Tsar, and most of us consider them sane, but just "dumb."

Gen. Gehlen and Gen. Vlassov formed what became the *Gehlenapparat,* the CIA's main source of info on Soviet affairs; Gehlen became the fulcrum of the CIA's "Soviet penetration" sector, working under James Jesus Angleton, Chief of Counter-Intelligence, breeder of prize orchids, lover of the arts, and a devout Roman Catholic.

Since the U.S. government based its foreign policies on C.I.A. reports, and the C.I.A. based its Soviet reports on Gehlen and some other former Nazis, plus a crew of Mystical Tsarists, as filtered and interpreted by a Papist intellectual, the U.S. government's ideas and actions became increasingly "weird," bizarre and frightening, in the view of the rest of the world. The results after 50 years seem very sad and very funny. In a nutshell, most of the world thinks we've gone batshit crazy. *"Tsarists and Nazis and spooks, oh my!"*

Although James Jesus Angleton was Gehlen's alleged supervisor, data indicates that the *Gehlenapparat* engaged in many activities, including kidnapping, extortion, murder, etc. about which Angleton either did not know or devoutly did not want to know.

But James J. Angleton seems a pathological case of some sort himself; he often hid his middle name because it revealed his half-Hispanic genes. An exceptionally intelligent and sensitive student of modern literature while at Yale, Angleton adored T.S. Eliot, Ezra Pound, Wallace Stevens, I.A. Richards, e e cummings and other SuperStars of Modernism; he met most of them personally. They collectively influenced Angleton's fascination with multiple perspectives, labyrinthine ambiguity and the eternal uncertainty of all inferences and "interpretations."

These modernist tendencies, which also appeared in science and philosophy at the same time, blossomed into obsessions and, perhaps, raging madness when Angleton systematically applied them to the spy-game. After all, modernism really dawned with Wilde's "The Reality of Masks" and Yeats's hermetic mystique that the world we know emerges from interactions of Mask, Anti-Mask, Self, and Anti-Self: which may or may not fit all of us or all the world but certainly fits the world of spooks and snoops that Angleton created.

Another C.I.A. officer, Edward Petty, described Angleton as "a lone wolf" and "a strange bird"; every other source I have found bluntly calls him "paranoid." He suspected everybody else in the C.I.A., and in "our" government generally, of being KGB moles, and operated with so much modernist ambiguity and hidden trapdoors that, in Petty's words, "nobody really knows" what plots he hatched most of the time. In short, he became as esoteric as the poets he admired, and remade the C.I.A. and, increasingly, our whole nation into a theatre of impenetrable mystery: a carnival Crazy House, an infinity of mirrors, a Chinese puzzle with no solution.

———

It's all in the mind.   — Ringo Starr

———

A.J. Weberman, a leading Kennedy assassination scholar, thinks Angleton personally organized the JFK hit, an idea also strongly hinted at by Norman Mailer's documentary novel, *Harlot's Ghost*, in which Angleton appears as "Hugh Montague." (Angleton's father was named Hugh; Angleton's code name was "Mother," and Montague's is "Harlot." Work on that, ye seekers of multiple meaning.)

If James Jesus really arranged the JFK assassination, he had probably decided that Kennedy was the top Soviet mole of all.

Why not? Angleton had Tsarist agents in all sorts of nooks of the Soviet system, and he knew the KGB had brains enough and energy enough to reciprocate by planting their own Masks and Anti-Masks in his own backyard, or maybe under his bed at night. According to Edward Jay Epstein, J.J.A.'s endless search for Soviet moles nearly destroyed the C.I.A. itself. Certainly, everybody in "the Company" learned to distrust everybody else.

Imagine a U.S. Caine with not one Queeg as captain, but a whole crew of Queegs, each worrying about what the others might be plotting. Angleton created that ship of shape-shifters in the C.I.A. and then, by osmosis, it spread through the government, evolving into the TSOG. As Henry Kissinger said, "Anybody in Washington who isn't paranoid must be crazy."

In short, the government cannot trust us because it can never know with absolute certainty what mischief we may hatch; and every sentence we speak into a bugged telephone may have as many possible meanings as Eliot's "The rose and the fire are one."

In William F. Buckley Jr.'s documentary novel, *Spytime: The Undoing of James Jesus Angleton,* occurs a scene that epiphanizes the TSOG's looped and relooped logic. Angleton and an associate discuss 17 or 37 possible interpretations of a bit of information (or disinformation) passed on by a possible Soviet defector (who might be a Soviet mole). At the end of the discussion, J.J.A. points out one more "reading" of the "text" that the associate hadn't considered: namely, that Angleton himself might be the top Soviet mole of all. You can't learn more about ambiguity and irony in a seminar on the poetry of William Empson.

In the same vein, after the death by drowning of "Montague" (Angleton) in *Harlot's Ghost,* the C.I.A. systematically investigates such alternative scenarios as: he's not dead and another water-rotted corpse has been foisted on them; or, the Soviets did it and have him full of truth serums already; or, he went over to the Soviets willingly; or, he was the cleverest of all traitors, working for the Reds all along.

"Trust No One," the motto of *X Files,* seems the only safe rule in the world Angleton created.

———

In any case, Angleton had an alliance with Italian fascists and the Mafia, dating from 1944 when he served as an O.S.S. officer in Italy. "Operation Gladio," a C.I.A. project to control Italian elections, was based on Angleton's fascist-Mafia connections, and employed techniques as varied as hiring Sophia Loren to do TV

commercials for politicians the C.I.A. liked, bribing liberal/left
politicos to move toward more right-wing positions, and employ-
ing the Mafia to assassinate some who couldn't be bribed, e.g.,
Prime Minster Aldo Moro.

In recruiting for Gladio, Angleton had a secret meeting with his
old friend Ezra Pound, in Genoa. Pound, under indictment for radio
broadcasts that he called "personal propaganda on behalf of the
U.S. Constitution" and which the Department of Justice called
"treason," did not get recruited into Gladio and instead spent 13
years in a hospital for the criminally insane, for expressing his
views about bankers and usury over the wrong radio station.

J.J.A. had better luck with a former Gestapo informant named
Licio Gelli, who formed a secret society called P2 within the
Grand Orient Lodge of Egyptian Freemasonry and eventually
infiltrated over 950 agents into the Italian government. Through P2
connections and Roberto Calvi, a P2 member and president of
Banco Ambrosiano in Milan, Gladio merged the Mafia's drug
laundering system with ongoing C.I.A. projects, using as screens
the Vatican Bank and 200 "ghost banks" which existed only in
Calvi's ledgers. The Tsarist-C.I.A.-Mafia chieftains then had
almost total control over both the multi-billion dollar illegal drug
business and the even more profitable anti-drug business.

It worked like this: among the 200 "ghost banks" that existed
only as postal drops, a few "real," or at least tangible, banks
existed. One, the Cisalpine Bank in the Bahamas, jointly owned by
Roberto Calvi of Banco Ambrosiano and Archbishop Paul "The
Gorilla" Marcinkus, served as the major funnel for money laundering. Its primary links were the Franklin National Bank, owned
by fellow Gladio asset Michele "The Shark" Sindona, and the
World Finance Corporation, owned and managed by eight
"former" (or allegedly "former") C.I.A. officers.

Cocaine profits generally went through the World Finance
Corporation, in Miami, and thence via Cisalpine, into the maze of
ghost banks, and thence through Ambrosiano and the Vatican to
numbered Swiss bank accounts. Heroin profits ran through the
Nyugun Hand Bank in Australia, also run by "former" C.I.A.
agents and thence into the same labyrinth. Some of the drug money

bought guns for terrorists and generally financed what *Washington Post* journalist Bob Woodward called "the undeclared wars of the C.I.A." The rest was sheer gravy, for those high in the TSOG, and it ran into billions a year for the Gladio group alone. Meanwhile, the TSOG drug cartel scored psycho-political gains as well as stuffing those numbered bank accounts. By flooding the U.S. with crack, they were able to create a mob hysteria that surpassed McCarthyism and now ranks beside the medieval witch-hunts; in the smoke and mirrors, only a few noticed that the Constitution had somehow gotten dismantled plank by plank.

As William S. Burroughs wrote 30 years ago, "Drug control is a thin pretext, and getting thinner, to increase police powers and to brand dissent as criminal." A voice crying in the wilderness...

Angleton was finally removed from the C.I.A. in 1974 when caught meddling in U.S. elections—something that the C.I.A. is only supposed to do in other countries. Calvi of Banco Ambrosiano was assassinated by the Mafia, for unknown reasons, in 1982. His secretary fell or was thrown out of her office window the same day Calvi was found hanged. Michele "The Shark" Sindona, another of the Gladio/P2/Mafia inner circle—remember?—was convicted of 64 counts of stock and currency fraud in New York, and of murdering a bank examiner in Rome; he was poisoned in prison while awaiting trial on other charges. Archbishop Paul "The Gorilla" Marcinkus was replaced as president of the Vatican Bank, when his role in Gladio drug-money laundering was revealed in the trials of lesser culprits, and later he got booted out of the Vatican entirely.

Licio Gelli stood trial for conspiracy but was acquitted. Later, evidence showed that Gelli was working for the KGB as well as the C.I.A.; which side he double-crossed most often remains unknown. But then, Gelli had worked for the Communist Underground in WWII, while also on the payroll of the Gestapo, and nobody claims to know which side he betrayed most often in that case either. Mask and Anti-Mask again...or, as T.S. Eliot wrote of a hippopotamus:

Though he looks so firm to us
He is only flesh and blood

Mino Pecorelli, the first journalist to expose Gladio/P2 infiltration of the Italian government, was killed on a street in Rome, shot through the mouth—the *sasso in bocca*, traditional Mafia punishment for informers. The same fate befell Sam Giancana, Mafia boss of Chicago, when subpoenaed by a congressional committee on assassinations—another *sasso in bocca*. Johnny Roselli, another Mafioso often involved in Tsarist/C.I.A. projects, simply disappeared when he got his subpoena. His body was found floating in a barrel in the Gulf of Mexico.

The major open functions of Mystical Tsarism now are the Drug Enforcement Administration (DEA) and the Food and Drug Administration (FDA). You all know about the DEA, its Piss Police and its vast army of snoops and informers—a vision to gladden the heart of Konstantin Pobedonostsev himself. The FDA operates similarly but with less publicity; it was described in these terms by Saul Kent of the Life Extension Foundation:

> The FDA's strong-arm tactics are used to intimidate and terrorize Americans into toeing their police-state line on health care and medicine. The FDA's purpose is not just to destroy the business and lives of their targets, but also to spread fear and terror throughout the land so that others…will remain weak and submissive.
>
>   [Source: http//www.livelinks.com/
>   sumeria/health/raids.html]

In 1957, the FDA burned all the books of dissident physician Wilhelm Reich, M.D., smashed his laboratory equipment with axes, and threw him in jail, where he died. In the 1960's, the DEA did the same kind of job on heretic psychologist Timothy Leary, Ph.D.

Lately, their major targets have been midwives, homeopaths, herbalists and physicians who offer safer and cheaper health care than the TSOG PharmCorps.

————

Although our first official and open Tsar was appointed during the brief, bloody reign of Bushware 1.0, the Tsar's powers only reached tyrannical status under Bill Clinton, a hillbilly relative of the royal Rockefellers. A former Tsar, General Barry McCaffrey, recently stated the theology of Mystic Tsarism in an article for the *Denver Post*. I condense a bit because, like most Tsars, Mac the Knife is a bit of a windbag:

> Each week, millions of Americans attend religious services to seek guidance, reaffirm moral values, offer charity and obtain a sense of community. Each of these four elements...requires us to guide them and teach them values. ...On May 10, I traveled to Colorado Springs to stand with Dr. James Dobson and the Young Life Christian Ministry. The ministry's youth programs are model efforts for how **faith-based organizations** can play a critical role in helping our young people choose the right path...[blah blah blah]... The One Way 2 Play program of the Fellowship of Christian Athletes is another example of how **faith groups** help young people... The One Way 2 Play program uses sports to teach the importance of a healthy lifestyle and a commitment to **faith**. ...As British Theologian Dean William Inge said: 'If we are to safeguard our children and communities, rabbis, priests, clerics, deacons, sisters, brothers and cantors must help lead the way'... [emphasis added]

Moronic faith and sheep-like docility are the bulwarks of Tsarism; any hint of scientific knowledge, rationality or even plain "horse sense" among the serfs are its major worries, and it blocks them every way it can. No Tsar will ever lavish such praise on scientists or other professional skeptics as McCaffery lavishes on the faithful and the sheep-herders who fleece and butcher them.

China is a big country with a lot of Chinese people living
there.
— Former French President Charles De Gaulle

And so, the Constitution in tatters, spies everywhere, we
inhabit "one nation under surveillance with wiretaps and mail
covers for all"; and everybody feels terrorized about whether their
houses and property will be seized next. In short, we find ourselves, as Trotsky found the Russians a century ago, midway
between European monarchism and Asiatic despotism.

It comes as no surprise that McCaffery stands accused of war
crimes, under the Nuremberg rulings. Bill Clinton may seem 77
kinds of sonofabitch, as most of us now agree, but nobody really
believes him a fool. When he picks a Tsar, he finds the right kind
of man for the job. The only way Bore or Gush can improve on
Mac the Knife is if, with further advances in genetic engineering,
they dig up the bones and clone the most famous, mystical and
murderous Tsar of them all—Ivan the Terrible, who alternated
between murdering masses of people and retiring to monasteries
for meditation and prayer.

Notes

For more info on the *Gehlenapparat*, see *The Yankee and
Cowboy War* by Carl Oglesby, Berkeley Medallion, NY, 1977; and
Everything Is Under Control by R.A. Wilson, Harper, NY, 1998.
The best overview of TSOG/C.I.A. operations in general is
Norman Mailer's docu-novel *Harlot's Ghost*, Random House, NY,
1991, in which Angleton appears as "Hugh Montague" and Gehlen
has a walk-on under his own name.

On the Gladio/P2 side of the TSOG, excellent books include *The Strange Death of God's Banker*, Foot and della Torre, Orbis, London, 1984; *The Calvi Affair*, by Larry Gurwin, Pan, London, 1984; *The Brotherhood*, by Stephen Knight, Grenada, London, 1984. The Calvi "ghost banks" and their strange links with real banks, including Chase Manhattan, are discussed amply in *In Banks We Trust*, Doubleday, NY, 1984, by Penny Lernoux, who leaves open the question of how many of the real banks were unwitting accomplices and how many knew what was going on and just kept mum while raking in the profits.

In God's Name, by David Yallop, Cape, London 1984, covers all this in greater depth, and also explores Licio Gelli's role in creating fake ID for Nazi war criminals, whom he later farmed out to the C.I.A. death squads. It also adds Pope John Paul I to the list of mysterious deaths involving the Vatican Bank, along with Pecorelli, Moro, Calvi, Roselli, Sindona et al.

My current acceptance that the Mafia killed Calvi (in previous writings I felt unsure) rests on the confession of Calogero Ganci, a Mafia hitman turned informant, who says he strangled Calvi himself. See *London Times*, 20 June 1996. Ganci was never told why the mob wanted "God's banker" dead; his job was to kill people, not to ask rude questions. Mrs. Calvi, the widow, still claims the orders came from the Vatican.

Our Tsar's war crimes are documented in "Overwhelming Force," by Seymour Hersh, *The New Yorker*, 22 May 2000.

Angleton's role as organizer of the JFK assassination is argued rather persuasively at http//weberman.com.

The best depth analysis of Mystical Tsarism remains T*he Mass Psychology of Fascism*, by Wilhelm Reich, M.D. Farrar, Strauss and Giroux, New York, 1970. Although Dr. Reich doesn't analyze Tsarism in particular, he relates Fascism to the dogmatic religions, faith in "leaders" ("little Fathers") and sexual misery of all the "Patriarchal Authoritarian" regimes throughout history, and his major bio-psychological theorems describe both Russian and American Tsarism as neatly as they fit the Holy Inquisition or

German-Italian Fascism. Vico's *New Science*, as cited above, will also repay close study.

Or—you can find most of this data, in one form or another by simply surfing the web. Set your search engine for "Rheinhold Gehlen," "Cisalpine Bank," "Licio Gelli," "Gladio" and all the other individual and group names in this synopsis, and you'll be astounded at how many Dirty Secrets are now open to the light of day.

THOUGHTS TO PONDER

The United States is not nearly so concerned that its acts be kept secret from its intended victims as it is that the American people not know of them.
— Former U.S. Attorney General Ramsey Clark

It IS as bad as you think, and they ARE out to get you

Government, in its best state, is but a necessary evil; in its worst state, an intolerable one; for when we suffer, or are exposed to the same miseries by a government, which we might expect in a country without a government, our calamity is heightened by reflecting that we furnish the means by which we suffer.
— Thomas Paine

A departure from principle in one instance becomes a precedent for a second; that second for a third; and so on, till the bulk of the society is reduced to be mere automatons of misery, to have no sensibilities left but for sin and suffering.
— Thomas Jefferson

BENEFITS OF FAITH-BASED ORGANIZATIONS

"Let the Fucking Junkies Die"

The Vatican has ruled that no Catholic organization should participate in programs involving legal injection of heroin, canceling all church involvement in needle exchange programs intended to prevent further spread of AIDS among heroin addicts. The Vatican's Congregation for the Doctrine of the Faith stated that legal heroin injections constitutes cooperation with "grave evil."

After which, they groped a few altar boys probably?

[Source: *Alcohol and Drug Abuse Weekly 10/2/2000*]

Moon Madness

ANKARA, Turkey—Turkish police recently arrested eight fookin' eejits for shooting guns at the moon during an eclipse.

A local Mullah said that shooting at the moon was an "irreligious" custom and urged the faithful only to pray to Allah during lunar eclipses.

Nobody in the area mentioned the scientific model of Earth-Sun-Moon orbits as a cause of the eclipse, or suggested that neither guns nor prayers would shorten the phenomenon.

[Source: Reuters]

Foot Magick

A campaign has been launched in Malaysia to try to protect women from being duped into having sex with randy shamans.

Twelve cases have been reported, four of them involving women who were told having sex with Holy Men would improve their businesses or bring back their straying husbands.

Dr. Ng Yen Yen says: "We believe there are many more cases which are not reported, particularly in rural areas."

She also cited the case of a medium called the Drunken Monk, who would cover himself in dirt, then wash his feet in brandy and water. Women devotees would drink the water, believing it was blessed.

[Source: http://www.pa.press.net/news/story/sm_3194.html]

IRISH MIST

Back in the 1980's, when I lived in the Environs of Howth Castle, a murder occurred in Phoenix Park and the police started looking for a suspect named James MacArthur. They found him living in the luxury pad of the Attorney General, which led to great scandal and outrage. The Attorney General was a bachelor in his 40s and MacArthur was a young man of about 20.

Even in puritanical Ireland, they have heard of Greek Love and certain inferences were discussed widely in the pubs, although not in the media. The AG resigned and the Prime Minister, Charles Haughey, had a press conference, in which nobody mentioned the un-Hibernian innuendoes going around, but the tension still got so great that Mr. Haughey accidentally had a slip of the tongue. None of the media repeated what Haughey had said, but the defense attorneys asked for a dismissal anyway because (they claimed) some prospective jurors might hear what the Head of Government had said and be prejudiced by it.

The judge ruled that there was no evidence of enough gossip to taint the jury pool, and MacArthur stood trial and was convicted. A year or so later I met a few reporters and learned what none of the media had dared to tell us: namely, that Haughey had inadvertently referred to MacArthur as "the murderer" instead of "the accused."

You see, the Irish media never pronounces on the guilt or innocence of accused persons. They consider that contrary to the ideas of fair trial and fair juries.

The same events could have happened in England, and perhaps in other civilized countries, although not in the U.S., where the media would have all proclaimed MacArthur's guilt from the day the coppers started hunting him as a suspect, and would have used banner headlines to announce that the head of government agreed with them that the guy really committed the murder.

I much prefer the rules governing criminal cases in civilized countries to the rules in the United States.

No, this is not another comment on O.J.—at least not in particular. I just don't like the lynch-mob stink that our media always emits when somebody gets accused of a major felony.

WORDS TO PONDER

Peace comes of communication.
— Ezra Pound, *Make It New*

Congress shall make no law abridging freedom of speech or of the press...
— Anon (allegedly found in some little-known historical document)

To live effectively is to live with adequate information.
— Norbert Weiner, *The Human Use of Human Beings*

An honest man can feel no pleasure in the exercise of power over his fellow citizens.
— Thomas Jefferson

Patriotism? Your patriotism waves a flag with one hand and picks pockets with the other!
— Ingrid Bergman to Cary Grant in *Notorious* (script by Ben Hecht)

DOG SODOMIZING SATANIC CHILD PORNOGRAPHERS!

BENEFITS OF FAITH-BASED ORGANIZATIONS

Sex, Satanism and Sodomized Dogs in Southern California

Ten little Indians going out to dine...

— Old Ballad

The Manhattan Beach Satanism/porno/child-abuse case has at last come to a climax, or at least a temporary anticlimax. After all the hysteria and hoopla about devil worship, a sodomized dog, other tortured animals, a "kiddie porn" industry in the schools, and assorted rites of Voodoo and Black Magic; after the closure of schools and the repeated vandalization of a church; after the ruin of dozens of careers and severe damage to hundreds of lives; the final tallies, as far as we can determine, run about as follows:

- Number of Manhattan Beach schools accused by rumor of having Satanic teachers during the original 1983 panic: 9.
- Number of churches similarly accused: 1.
- Total number of institutions accused: (9 + 1) = 10.

Additional charges originally circulated:

- "An AWOL Marine sodomized the dog of one of the molested children!"
- "Teachers at the nine schools belonged to a child pornography ring!"
- "Teachers also belonged to a Satanic cult!"

53

• "The cult existed not only in Manhattan Beach and nearby towns but throughout the United States!"
• "Animal mutilations and bloody sacrifices occurred in all local schools and at one local Protestant church, St. Cross Episcopal in Hermosa Beach!!"
• "Hundreds of children had suffered molestation or had unwillingly participated in Satanic rituals!!"
• "Heavy Metal Rock caused it all; if you play certain records backwards, you can hear voices saying 'Satan is my Master!!!'"

Additional interesting information:

• Number of teachers accused of child molestation and/or Satanic rituals: No exact figure can be found now, but somewhere in the neighborhood of one hundred.
• Mental status of original complaining witness: Previously judged paranoid schizophrenic by psychiatrists; at the time she made the charges, receiving Welfare on grounds of continued paranoid schizophrenia.
• Number of Manhattan Beach institutions at which the District Attorney finally decided enough evidence existed to indict suspects: one out of the 9 schools (the McMartin Pre-School), or 11.1%. Including the church, one out of the 10 institutions, or 10.0%.
• Number of schools at which evidence to indict was deemed insufficient by District Attorney: 8 out of 9 (88.9%).
• Number of institutions at which evidence was deemed insufficient to indict: 9 out of 10 (90.0%)
• Fate of the 8 schools at which prosecutors found insufficient evidence to indict: Due to public hostility, all 8 closed down and never re-opened.
• Fate of the McMartin school: Sold to pay legal expenses of defendants.
• Disposition of the alleged "Satanic" St. Cross Episcopal church: No evidence to indict found by D.A.; however,

under harassment and death threats, the pastor closed the church and moved to another part of the country.
• Evidence of Satanic rituals considered by the D.A. strong enough to bring into court: None (0.0%).
• Evidence of a "child pornography ring" strong enough to bring into court: None. (0.0%).

And then there were seven...

• Number of original defendants indicted for child molestation: 7, out of the nearly 100 originally accused by rumor (approximately 7.0%).
• Approximate ages of said defendants: An elderly woman, her middle-aged daughter, her 20ish grand-daughter and grand-son, three youngish female teachers.
• Genders of these defendants: 6 female (85.7%), one male (Ray Buckey; 14.3%).
• Number of offenses alleged by the State against 7 defendants: 208 counts of child molestations, 0 counts of Satanism, 0 counts of pornography.
• Disposition of Satanism/animal mutilation rumors: After initial 1983 investigation, regarded as an embarrassment by police and D.A., who not only would not bring this matter into court but prefer not to discuss it anymore; said Satanist cult still widely believed in by some people who call radio talk shows regularly to protest alleged police "cover-up."
• Disposition of original 7 defendants: Charges of molestation dropped for lack of evidence: 5 cases (71.4%); charges actually brought to trial: 2 cases (28.5%).
• These percentages as calculated against all those originally accused by rumor:

— Nearly 95 cases never arrested = approximately 95%.
— Five cases arrested but not brought to court for lack of evidence = approximately 5%.
— Two cases brought to trial = approximately 2% of all teachers originally accused. (Total equals 102% because exact figure on all accused in 1983 not available.)

And then there were two...

• Of 208 original charges against two remaining suspects, number of charges finally considered strong enough to bring into court: 53 (20.6%).

• Charges against these two remaining defendants dropped for lack of evidence: 155 (89.4%).

• Fate of original prosecutor, Glen Stevens: He became convinced of the innocence of both defendants and resigned; now sells real estate.

• Opinion of Ira Reiner before he was elected D.A. and took over prosecution of the two defendants: Told newspapers the case against all defendants was "incredibly weak."

• Time the jury deliberated in first trial: 9 weeks.

• Reasons jury gave for not believing child witnesses: Films of interrogation appeared to jury to show children being coached or coaxed into saying what the investigators wanted to hear. Some children had lapses of memory while testifying.

• Result of first trial: Defendant Peggy McMartin Buckey, acquitted on all charges (100%); Defendant Ray Buckey, acquitted on 40 charges (75.4%); jury deadlocked on 13 charges (24.6%).

• Number of defendants then remaining still legally accused out of approximately 100 originally accused by rumor: One, or approximately 1%. (Ray Buckey.)

• Percentage of all accused teachers not brought to court for lack of evidence or not believed guilty by jury: 99%.

And then there was one...

• Disposition of remaining 13 charges against Buckey: 5 dropped by D.A. Reiner (38.4%); 8 brought into court in Ray Buckey's second trial. (62.6% of remaining charges, or 3.8% of all original charges against him, or 0.0038% of all charges against all teachers.)

- Medical examiners who testified to finding physical evidence of molestation in alleged victims: 1. (25% of all medical examiners testifying).
- Medical examiners who testified to finding no physical evidence of molestation: 3. (75% of all medical examiners testifying).
- Last official act of second jury before declaring deadlock: Rereading all medical testimony.
- Time the jury deliberated in second trial before reaching deadlock: 15 days.
- Reasons given by jury for not believing child witnesses: Films convinced them children had been coaxed or coached into making charges. One child repudiated former charges while on witness stand and announced she could not remember what happened.
- Result of Buckey's second trial: Mistrial declared.
- Poll of jurors on the 8 remaining charges about which they deadlocked:

    — Majority wanted acquittal on 6 charges, but could not convince minority.
    — Even split on 7th charge; majority wanted conviction on the one remaining charge of the original 208 charges against him (0.47%, somewhat less than one-half of 1%), but could not convince minority that Buckey was guilty "beyond a reasonable doubt."

And then there were none...

- Result for Ray Buckey: He has, due to high bail, served more time in prison (five years) than anybody actually convicted of child molestation in California in this generation, although he has not been convicted of any crime.
- Result for Peggy Buckey, mother of Ray: although eventually acquitted of all charges, she served two years in prison awaiting trial.
- Results for others:

— One of the original suspects died of a deliberate or accidental drug overdose.

— One accuser died of alcoholism.

— One defense investigator committed suicide.

• Alleged hope (according to political pundits) of District Attorney Ira Reiner in fighting this "incredibly weak" and increasingly diminishing case for so long, with less and less charges (from 208 to 53 to 8) against fewer and fewer defendants (from nearly 100 to seven to two to one lone man): Mr. Reiner hoped to become State Attorney General.

• Result of Mr. Reiner's alleged hope: He did not win the nomination for Attorney General. He has declined to bring Ray Buckey to trial a third time.

• Cost to the taxpayers:

— According to *Los Angleles Times,* more than $14,000,000 for the trials.

— Cost of keeping Ray Buckey in prison five years, and Peggy Buckey in prison two years: not known to this author.

The Sequel...

• One hour after the judge declared a mistrial in the second Buckey case, the Radical Feminist talk-show host Carol Hemingway (KGIL, Los Angeles) placed Mr. Buckey on trial again, beginning proceedings by declaring "I believe the children." Two agents of the prosecution appeared on this show; nobody from the defense appeared. Ms. Hemingway, after 28 minutes (by my watch) of this one-sided testimony, repeated her original verdict: "I believe the children."

• Ambiguity of Ms. Hemingway's verdict: She never specified if she believed only the children's charges against Buckey, or their charges against the seven original defendants, or their charges against virtually all Manhattan Beach teachers during the original 1983 panic.

- Audience reaction to Ms. Hemingway's extra-legal "trial": After hearing the case for the prosecution and not getting confused (like the juries in the two trials) by the case for the defense, all callers but one lone heretic agreed with Ms. Hemingway's "pro-child" verdict and pronounced Buckey guilty.
- Ms. Hemingway's response to the one lone heretic who claimed the children had been manipulated by adult hysteria: Ms. Hemingway described him as "sick, sick, sick!"
- Graffiti reported on McMartin Pre-School:

RAY MUST DIE

- Movie that opened in Manhattan Beach the day of declared mistrial of Ray Buckey: *Presumed Innocent,* starring Harrison Ford.
- Source of title of said movie: An ancient Anglo-Saxon legal principle unknown to Ms. Hemingway and most inhabitants of Manhattan Beach.

I haven't committed a crime. What I did was fail to comply with law.
— David Dinkins, New York City Mayor, answering accusations that he failed to pay his taxes.

- Statement of said ancient Anglo-Saxon legal principle: An accused is presumed innocent until proven guilty beyond a reasonable doubt.

• Reasons adduced by local residents for not according Ray Buckey this traditional presumption of innocence even after 24 jurors, pouring over the evidence for 11 weeks and one day, failed to find enough evidence to convict him of anything:

— "There's no smoke without fire."
— "It can't all have been hysteria."
— "The police never arrest an innocent man."
— "I believe the children."

• Fate of Peggy, sister of Ray Buckey: Fired from her job with Orange County; regained it after prolonged legal battle.

• Fate of Peggy, mother of Ray Buckey: Sued the State for malicious prosecution, on grounds that officials knew original complaining witness:

— (a) suffered mental illness, and
— (b) had filed false crime reports before.

• Results of this suit: Judge ruled against Mrs. Buckey; case under appeal.

• Fate of five others arrested but never brought to trial:

— All lost their jobs and reputations.
— All have filed suit against the State, charging malicious prosecution.
— All have lost in original trials.
— All cases under appeal.

• Reaction of one (unaccused) teacher who called Michael Jackson talk show (KABC): As coach of a girl's basketball team, he announced he intended in the future to have a female teacher present at all training sessions.

• Lapse of logic of said teacher: He forgot that in the original indictment, Ray Buckey was alleged to have performed molestations while two or more female teachers were present and assisting in said molestations.

• Summary for those confused by excess detail:

— Years spent by the State trying to convict at least some teachers of some crime: 7.

— Money spent in this endeavor: Between $14 million and $20 million.
— Teachers actually convicted: None (0.0%).
• Location of the dog-sodomizing Marine:
— Never seen by anyone but the paranoid schizophrenic who started all this.
— Never found by police.
— Never heard of again.
• Disposition of allegedly sodomized dog: Unknown.

[Sources: *Santa Monica Outlook*, 29 July and 7 August, 1990;
Los Angeles Times, 28 and 29 July 1990;
Carol Hemingway Show, KGIL, 27 July 1990, 2–4 pm;
Michael Jackson[1] Show, KABC, 28 July 1990, 10–11 am]

Postscript

After I wrote "Sex, Satanism and Sodomized Dogs," the new witch-hysteria continued to escalate all over the country. It finally seemed to reach the point where the tiny minority of us that the "experts" could not induce to "remember" Satanic molestations and cannibalistic rituals, UFO abductions, or at least run-of-the-mill incest, seemed an increasingly microscopic part of the population.

Many "experts" explained, lamely, that we few unmolested people simply suffer from a collective amnesia brought on by horrors too awful for the mind to recall. This total forgetting of alleged years of hellish terror even has a "scientific" (or "pseudo-scientific"?) name now: "robust repression."

Curiously, in the case of the best-documented atrocity of the 20th century—Hitler's Holocaust—not one recorded victim has suffered from "robust repression." The survivors all remember very well every horror they saw, and none of them ever needs hypnosis or psychological suggestion to help them "remember"

---

[1] The Los Angeles radio talk-show host with a British accent, not the singer/alleged child molester. [Ed.]

(much to the annoyance and inconvenience of Holocaust revision-
ists). People only seem to suffer this mysterious "robust repression" when confronted by Satanists, UFOnauts, or inconvenient
fathers (blokes that their mothers want to dump after first hitting
them hard in the divorce court).
Odd, wouldn't you say?

———»●«———

> If you ordered a boxcar full of sons-of-bitches, and I
> showed up, you could consider the order filled.
>
> — Robert Mitchum

———»●«———

In *Satanic Panic* (Open Court, Chicago, 1993), sociologist
Jeffrey Victor of Jamestown Community College has recorded 62
"rumor panics" similar to the McMartin case in the past decade.
Many have involved the FBI's Behavioral Science Unit, which has
repeatedly dug and dug and *dug* in the alleged sites of the "mass
graves" of these Satanic groups and found not one skeleton.
Not even a shin-bone.
Not even the intercostal clavical that Cary Grant pursued so
frantically all through *Bringing Up Baby*.
Kenneth Lamming of the Behavioral Science Unit finally
announced, after digging in all those empty graves, that the FBI
has found no evidence of an existing Satanic cult that performs
human sacrifices. Naturally, Radical Feminists and Fundamentalists denounced him as an agent of "the cover-up."
This total lack of real evidence has led to some re-examination
of the new witch-hunt. The False Memory Syndrome Foundation,
with over 3,700 members, both psychologists and laypersons, has
gotten publicity in most of the media, producing many cases where
the accuser later recanted. The FMSF has also produced reams of
evidence from clinical tests showing that people under hypnosis
will "remember" anything the hypnotist wants them to remember.

The New Yorker for May 17 and May 24, 1993, presented, in detail, the case of an accused Satanic child molester who, under persistent questioning, gradually admitted he "remembered" all the atrocities alleged against him, including defecating on his daughter after raping her. Then a psychologist demonstrated that this poor weak-minded guy would also "remember" anything, however absurd or impossible, that the psychologist invented and told him his accusers had charged against him.[2] Similar exposes of the "persistence of false memory" have received wide publicity in the media—including Ann Landers' column and the Donohue show on TV.

True Believers, however, still believe truly. *MS.* magazine declared its Faith in Satanic Child Abuse cults a decade ago and no Radical Feminist will disagree with *MS.,* the Holy Scripture of their dogma. A Ms. Linda Napolitano still appears at UFO conventions telling how UFOnauts sexually assaulted her and two C.I.A. agents tried to drown her after she revealed the horrible details. (Apparently, the C.I.A. doesn't know how to drown somebody, although they have a damned impressive record of assassinating heavily-guarded leaders of unpopular nations...)

And a chap named David Huggins goes around selling paintings he has made of several female UFOnauts who have sexually molested him. If you want to see a voluptuous *Playboy*-like version of the "monsters" in bad sci-fi, some of Mr. Huggins' paintings appear in the May 15, 1993, issue of a cynical journal called *Saucer Smear* (PO Box 1704, Key West FL 33041). The editor, a

---

[2] A mildly retarded fellow named Whitmore confessed to a murder in New York, back in the early 1960s, and later evidence proved him totally innocent. This led to the Supreme Court ruling that a suspect must have an opportunity to obtain legal counsel before the police work him over, a rule later made more stringent in the more famous Miranda case. In both the Whitmore case and the above "Satanism" case, no evidence of police brutality or torture, etc., ever appeared. Nor did anybody hypnotize these persons. Some low-self-esteem types will evidently confess to anything if the police insist on their guilt often enough and loud enough. See my *Cosmic Trigger II* (New Falcon Publications) for an Irish case in which a whole family confessed to a crime which forensic evidence proved they had not committed.

wonderfully witty fellow named Jim Moseley, has met Huggins and says he thinks Huggins really believes his own yarns.

Why not? Thousands, or tens of thousands, of horny men in the Medieval Age believed female demons had siphoned off their seed in the night...

IN LOVING MEMORY OF THE DEAD...

Some may think I regard the Constitution as an almost sacred text. Not at all: I admit it has a few defects and blemishes. I just consider it a hell of a lot better than the system we have now.

The TSOG officially buried the last bleedin' and ragged remnants of the Constitution under Bushware 2.0. with something called the USA PATRIOT Act, thereby fulfilling Huey Long's famous prediction that if fascism ever came to America it would call itself Americanism.

Of course, according to the official story, Dubya only put the Constitution in a kind of cryonic suspension for four years and then will wave a magic wand and revive it.

Anybody who believes that resurrection yarn has indeed attained True Faith, and ranks as a loyal serf of Tsarism.

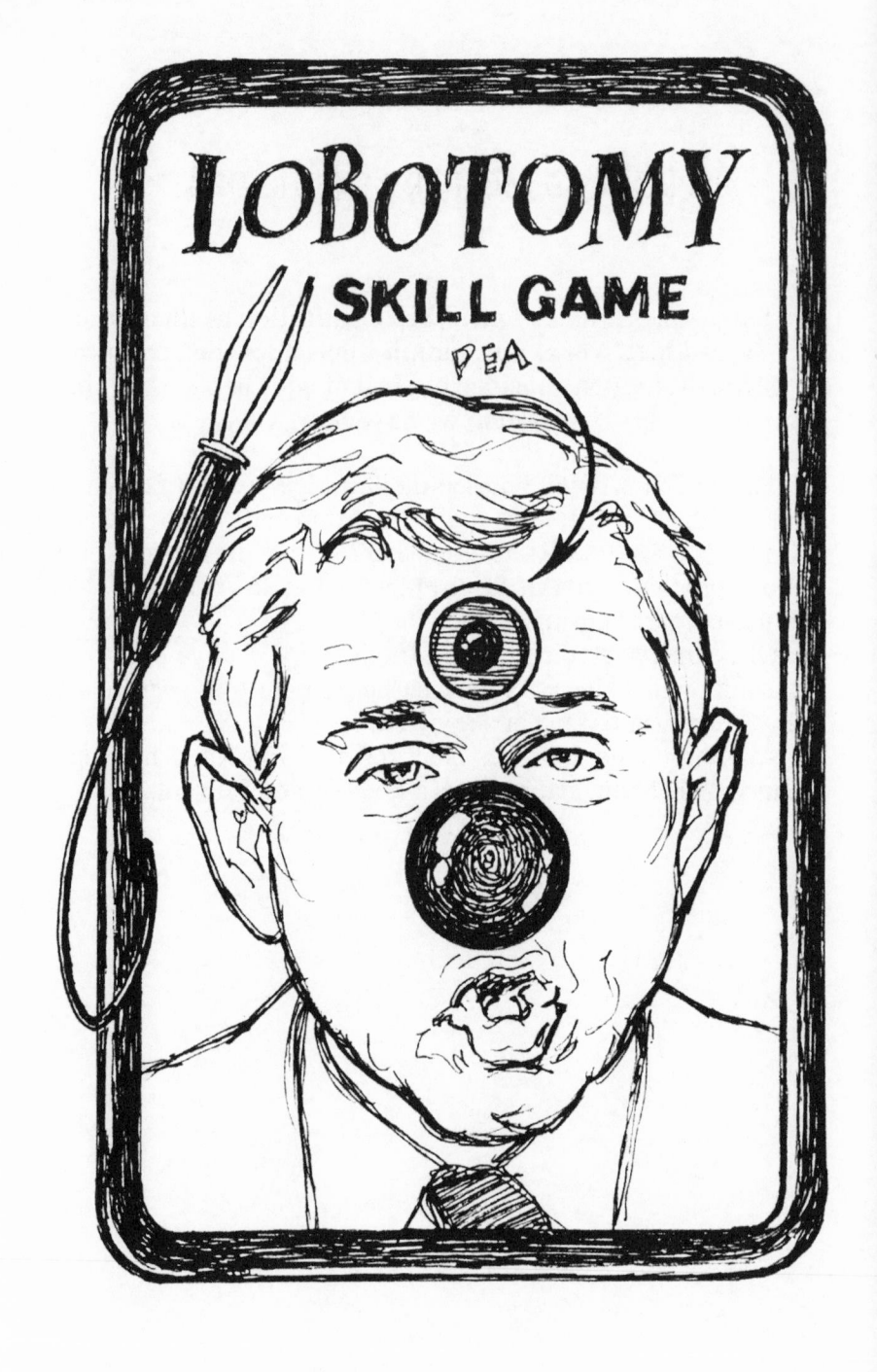

HOW TO GET IN TROUBLE

Not that a person who defends the Constitution is a criminal or terrorist, or a person who asks you, 'Why did you stop me' may be a terrorist, but certain things, I don't want to use the word common, certain characteristics that these people who were legitimately investigated reflect it.

— Ed Hall, Federal Bureau of Investigation

WARNING!
WARNING!
WARNING!

WILSON DESCRIBES himself as a 'guerrilla ontologist,' signifying his intention to **attack** thought and language the way terrorists **attack** their targets: to jump out from the shadows for an unprovoked **attack,** then slink back and hide behind a hearty belly laugh.

— Pope Robert Sheaffer,
The Skeptical Inquirer, Spring 1990

---

the
Farben
works
still
intact

WHO OWNS USCORP?

Corporations that have donated at least $500,000 to both Bore and Gush:

Enron
AFLAC
Amer Airlines
Amer Express
Amer Financial Group
Amer Home Products
Amer Intl. Group
America Online
Anheuser-Busch
Archer Daniels Midland
AT&T
Atlantic Richfield Co.
Bacardi Martini USA
Bechtel Group
Bell Atlantic
BellSouth
Blue Cross & Blue Shield
Boeing
Boston Capital Partners
Bristol-Myers Squibb
Chevron
Circus Circus
Citigroup
Coca-Cola
Eli Lilly & Co.
Entertainment
Ernst & Young
Exxon Mobil
Federal Express

Flo-Sun Sugar Co.
General Dynamics
General Electric
Georgia-Pacific
Intl. Game Technology
Joseph E. Seagram & Sons
Limited Inc.
Lockheed Martin
Loews Corp.
MBNA Corp.
MCI Worldcom
MGM Grand
Microsoft
Mirage Resorts
New York Life Insurance
Northern Telecom
Ocean Spray Cranberries
Oracle
Owens Corning
Pacific Gas & Electric
Paine Webber
Park Place
Pfizer
Philip Morris
Prudential Insurance
Rite Aid
SBC Communications
Schering-Plough
Sprint

Sunoco	United Technologies
Time Warner	Upjohn
Union Pacific	US West
United Airlines	Walt Disney
United HealthCare	

Now, folks, who do you think will win the election? Or does it really matter a damn?

[Source: Jim Hightower, http://www.jimhightower.com/]

O.J. AGONISTES

Racism designates the ignorant, bigoted, politically incorrect dogma that O.J. must "be guilty" because he "is" black.

Radical Feminism designates the enlightened, educated, politically correct dogma that O.J. must "be guilty" because he "is" male.

Please note carefully the important difference between these dogmas. Please ignore the overwhelming similarity between them, or you will become—ah, um—unfashionable.

Neurosemantics

Some readers probably think I oppose Feminism and believe O.J. Simpson was innocent.

Such readers need to study logic and general semantics.

I enthusiastically support most of Feminism and do not claim to know enough about the evidence to have a strong opinion about O.J.'s innocence or his guilt. To quote Korzybski,

I have said what I have said;
I have not said what I have not said.

BENEFITS OF FAITH-BASED ORGANIZATIONS

Santa's Claws

As Weston le Barre pointed out a long time ago,
in his classic *Ghost Dance: Origins of Religion*,
from the bottom of South America up over
North America and over the North Pole
and down across most of Europe and Asia,
remnants can be found of a primordial bear-god.

Nine years ago, in Burlington, North Carolina, a group of decent, Christian, hard-working folks who called themselves the Truth Tabernacle Church, held a trial featuring the well-known elf, Santa Claus, as defendant.

They charged Mr. Claus, represented in court by a stuffed dummy, with all sorts of high crimes and misdemeanors. They charged him with paganism. They charged him with perjury (for claiming to be Saint Nicholas). They even charged him with encouraging child battering by appearing in whiskey ads. Worse yet, they found him guilty on all counts, for basically being a jolly old elf—i.e., a pagan god trying to steal Christmas from Christ.

It wasn't the first time Mr. Claus got the boot from a Christian congregation. Pope John XXIII threw the suspiciously merry old troll out of the Holy Roman Catholic and Apostolic church back in the late 1960's. The Jehovah's Witnesses have always denounced Santa for his unsavory pagan past. (They also recognized Christmas trees as phallic symbols even before Freud.) Many Fundamentalists believe that all pagan gods are basically one false god—the same demon in different disguises—and they think the disguise is thin in the case of this particular elf. It only takes a minor letter switch, they point out, to reveal Santa Claus as SATAN Claus.

73

I sort of think the Fundies have it right for once. Santa not only has an unsavory pagan ancestry but a rather criminal family history all around. Let me Illuminize you...

As Weston le Barre pointed out a long time ago, in his classic *Ghost Dance: Origins of Religion,* from the bottom of South America up over North America and over the North Pole and down across most of Europe and Asia remnants can be found of a primordial bear-god. You can find this deity in cave paintings from southern France carbon-dated at 30,000 BC. You can find him and her (for this god is bisexual) disguised in Artemis and Arduina and King Arthur, all unmasked via canny detective work by folklorists (and etymologists—who first spotted the bear-god when they identified the Indo-European root *ard,* bear). You can track the bear-god in dwindling forms in a hundred fairy tales from all over Europe and Asia. And you can find the rituals of this still-living god among the surviving indigenous tribes of both American continents.

———⟫●⟪———

I'm not going to have some reporters pawing through our papers. We are the president.
— Hillary Rodham Clinton commenting on the release of subpoenaed documents.

———⟫●⟪———

And Santa, like Peter Pan and the Green Man of the spring festivals and the Court Jester and (in an odd way) Chaplin's beloved Little Tramp—all, all have traits of the god that walks like a man and acts nasty sometimes and clownish sometimes and who was ritually killed and eaten by most of our ancestors in the Stone Age, who then became one with their god and thus also became (if the ritual worked) as brave as their god. See Sir James Frazer's *Golden Bough* for gory details.

—————

And I swear the same God-Bear tromps and shambles through every page of Joyce's masterpiece of psycho-archeology, *Finnegans Wake*; and if you don't believe me, consult Adaline Glasheen's *Third Census to "Finnegans Wake."*

Most folklorists recognize "the cannibal in the woods" as a humanized relic of the bear-god. The heroine, in 101 tales, meets him while on a mission of mercy. He generally sets the heroine to solve three riddles, and when she succeeds, instead of eating her he becomes her ally and helps her reach her goal. One variation on that became *The Silence of the Lambs*. Another became Little Red Riding Hood.

What? Hannibal Lecter another of Santa's uncouth family?

Yes, indeed.

In some rustic parts of Europe and probably in Kansas, Santa retains traces of his carnivorous past. Children are told that if they are "good" all year, Santa will reward them, but if they are "bad" he will EAT THEM ALL UP. (Yeah, the Boogie Man or Bogie or Pookah or Puck are all of somewhat ursine ancestry, although other animal-gods got mixed in sometimes.)

As Crazy Old Uncle Ezra wrote in Canto 113:

> The gods have not returned. "They have never left us."

Jung might state the case thusly: gods, as archetypes of the genetic human under-soul (or "collective unconscious"), cannot be killed or banished; they always return with a new mask but the same symbolic meaning.

Related example: young ladies in ancient Greece were often seduced or raped by satyrs; in the Arab lands, we note a similar outbreak of randy djinni; in India, it was devas. In the Christian Dark Ages, it began happening to young men, too, especially to monks. They called the lascivious critter an incubus. Now it's happening all around us, and the molesters come from Outer Space. The sex-demon, like the Great Mother and the Shadow and our ursine hero, and the three brothers hunting the dragon (recognize them in *Jaws*? spot them doing their Three Stooges gig?): these archetypal forces always come back under new names. Sir Walter Scott called them "the crew that never rests."

And the bear-god seems wakeful lately. He has appeared prominently in four recent movies (*Clan of the Cave Bear, Legends of the Fall, The Edge, The Bear*) and snuck into Modern Lit 101 not only via Joyce but also via Faulkner's great parable, "The Bear." He also pops up to deliver the punch-line in Norman Mailer's *Why Are We in Vietnam?*

We will see more of him, methinks.

———⟫●⟪———

Meanwhile, Santa, the Jester/Clown/Fertility God aspect of Father Bear, is doing quite well also despite getting the bum's rush by some grim, uptight Christers. He has quite successfully stolen Xmas from X and brings pagan lust and pagan cheer to most of us, every year, just when we need it most, in the dead of winter. His beaming face appears everywhere and if we have a minor cultural war going on between those who wish to invoke him via alcohol and those who prefer their invocations per cannabis, we all share the pagan belief, at least for part of a week, that the best way to mark the solstice and the year's dying ashes is to form a loving circle and all get bombed together.

As a pagan myself, I wouldn't have it any other way.

———⟫●⟪———

Think SMALL and yo rob a gas
STATION
Thing BIG and yo PresiDENT of the
NATION
                              — Tangerine Dream

THOUGHTS TO PONDER

I don't know if God exists, but it would be better for His reputation if He didn't.

— Jules Renard

Following the path of least resistance is what makes rivers and men crooked.

— Anonymous

BELINDA: Ay, but you know we must return good for evil.
LADY BRUTE: That may be a mistake in the translation.

— Sir John Vanbrugh, *The Provoked Wife*

WAR ON *SOME* DRUGS

I suggest a simple neurosemantic experiment. Every time you hear the expression "the war on drugs," change it mentally to "the war on **some** drugs." After all, the only ones who seem *"at war" with **all** drugs* are the Christian Scientists and they fight non-violently (via boycott).

At the same time call up to mind all the Drug Stores and Bars/Saloons in your town or neighborhood and all the cigarette shelves in your friendly supermarket and remember that the government has started no war against them. When you understand that we have no "war on drugs" but only a "war on *some* drugs," consult the passages on double-think and duck-speak in Orwell's *1984* for further neurolinguistic illumination.

The Piss Police

And the Beast said,
"By their pee shall ye judge them,
And by your pee shall ye be judged,
And all shall be judged by their pee,
And in the snow shall their names be written."
　　　— Abdul Alhazred, *The TSOGonomicon*

Poison from the Sky

The TSOG sometimes tries to justify prohibition by comparing tabu drugs to poison and suggesting that they are attempting to keep "poison" out of communities. Actually, the drug war itself is spreading real poison into some places where people live.

The *New York Times* recently reported on the environmental devastation caused by pesticide allegedly used to eradicate illegal drug crops in Colombia. While crop spraying is often touted as a method to stop drugs, the destruction caused to humans and other animals is catastrophic.

An American embassy official claimed, "Being sprayed on certainly does not make people sick," but he did not offer to drink a glass of malathion to prove his Faith.

[Source: *DrugSense FOCUS Alert* #171 May 3, 2000]

For Felons Only

Washington politicians always end every discussion...by spreading herbicides that may ruin agricultural lands for years.

— Carlos Ball, publisher

NOTHING TO FEAR

I have lost several friends and colleagues in the last couple of years (Leary and Burroughs are only the most famous ones), and it has finally really dawned on me that I don't just qualify as "getting older"; I qualify as old, period. Now another friend has cancer, and yet another has had a series of massive strokes, and two more just died in a month.

I'm glad I have a lot of young friends, because the old ones are all leaving me.

Burroughs wrote a lot about preparing for the Big Sleep by getting out of your body while still alive, via Tibetan and Egyptian methods. Leary also tried those methods (aided by a Lilly isolation tank) and may or may not have had his head preserved cryonically, depending on whose story you believe. I don't regard either of these ideas as preposterous or silly: since I know nothing for sure, nothing seems really unthinkable.

Death makes me realize how deeply I have internalized the agnosticism I preach in all my books. I consider dogmatic belief and dogmatic denial very childish forms of conceit in a world of infinitely whirling complexity. None of us can see enough from one corner of space-time to know "all" about the rest of space-time.

Every day seems full of wonderments to me: Death will probably come to me as the greatest wonderment of all.

As some Roman wrote,

> Nothing to clutch in life,
> Nothing to fear in death

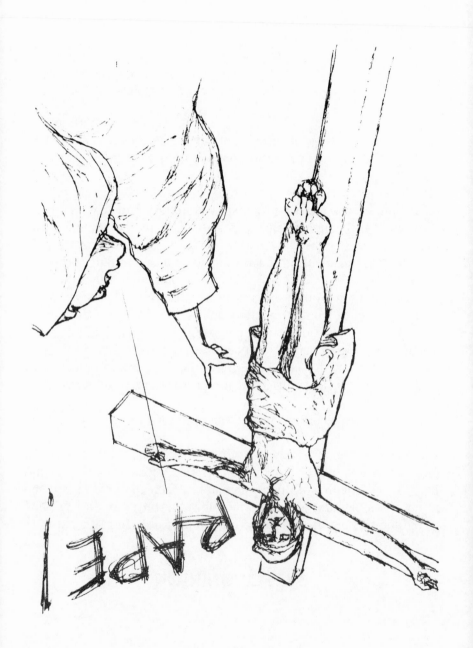

"POTENTIAL" CRIMINALS

I glanced into *alt.feminazis* today and found a lively debate about whether the Radical Feminist claim that "all men are potential rapists" leads to the conclusion "Jesus was a potential rapist." (It does. See Aristotle's *Logic*, part one, or Boole's *Laws of Thought*. If all **m** are **pr**, and **j** is an **m**, than **j** is **pr**; i.e., if all men are potential rapists and Jesus was a man, then Jesus was a potential rapist.)

I think this issue arouses so much fury because people are not aware that group-hate has never really become unfashionable. Only the target groups ever change. Thus, the Ku Klux Klan's dogma "All black men are potential rapists" seems ignorant, awful and politically incorrect, because it targets a group now on the "unfashionable to hate" list. The RadiFemi "all men are potential rapists" seems enlightened, educated and politically correct because it targets a group now on the "fashionable to hate" list.

You must always hate the right group to maintain your modernity. To become post-modern, find even more groups to hate.

Only idiots like Jesus (a potential rapist) and Buddha (another of that ilk) ever proposed living without hate of any groups... Oh, and the neurolinguist Korzybski, who described group hatreds as semantic hallucinations symptomatic of what he called "unsanity". But he "was" another potential rapist. Just substitute **k** for **j** above...

SCHROEDINGER'S JEW

Ninety-seven years ago today, Leopold Bloom, a fictitious man, wandered the streets of Dublin, a real city; and Joyce scholars still argue about his odd odyssey. I would like to add to the confusion with a note about Bloom's "Jewishness."

"Is" Leopold Bloom a Jew?

Not according to Orthodox Rabbinical law, which defines a Jew as the child of a Jewish mother. Bloom, as the child of a Protestant mother, "is not" a Jew.

According to Nazi law, however, a Jew "is" a person with a known Jewish ancestor. Bloom, as the son of Rudolph Bloom (born Rudolph Virag), "is" a Jew.

See how easily a person can "be" and "not be" a Jew at the same time?

On the third hand, most humanists define a Jew as one who believes in and practices the Judaic religion. By this definition, Bloom who neither believes in nor practices any religion "is not" a Jew. But Marilyn Monroe, who practiced and probably tried to believe in Judaism while married to Arthur Miller, "was" a Jew by that definition—for those few years, if not before or after.

Extensionally or phenomenologically, a Jew "is" somebody considered Jewish by all or most of the people he meets. By this standard the multi-ordinal Bloom "is" a Jew again.

Once more: In terms of pure existentialism a Jew "is" somebody who *chooses* to consider themselves Jewish. Bloom obviously doesn't consider himself Jewish, but Irish—most of the time. Only when under verbal assault by the anti-semitic Citizen in Barney Kiernan's pub does Bloom define himself as Jewish ("And

Jesus was a Jew too. Your god. He was a Jew like me.") Here he obviously has in mind the "known Jewish ancestor" rule, because he adds "And so was his father," to which the Citizen replies, as a correct Catholic, "He had no father," and Bloom, unfamiliar with that theology—Aristotelian logic played with deuces, eights and one-eyed jacks wild—can only pragmatically reply, "Well, his uncle then."

But recalling the incident later, Bloom says "And he called me a Jew, which as a matter of fact I'm not." Here he returns to his customary "believer in Judaic religion" definition.

I suppose Joyce made Bloom such a tangled genetic and cultural mixture to expose the absurdities of anti-Semitism; but I also suspect that he wanted to undermine that neurolinguistic habit which postmodernists call "essentialism" and which Korzybski claimed invades our brains and causes hallucinations or delusions every time we use the word "is."

DITZ DELUXE
PARTY DOLL
ACTION
MOTION
LOOKS
UNBELIEVABLY
REAL

THOUGHTS TO PONDER AGAIN

The means of defense against foreign danger historically have become the instruments of tyranny at home.

— James Madison

Good intentions will always be pleaded for any assumption of power. The Constitution was made to guard the people against the dangers of good intentions. There are men in all ages who mean to govern well, but they mean to govern. They promise to be good masters, but they mean to be masters.

— Daniel Webster

Whenever I watch TV and see those poor starving kids all over the world, I can't help but cry. I mean, I'd love to be skinny like that but not with all those flies and death and stuff.

— Mariah Carey

KEEP YOUR SENSE OF HUMOR

Our legal system is a giant practical joke and my law
school diploma is a whoopee cushion.
> — "Zoe Clemens", *LA Law*

"Beating Them with Rods"...

According to Bill Clinton's position on medical marijuana,
only the Federal Government has the right to decide how much
pain we must endure in illness or dying.

We do not have that right, nor do our families or doctors, nor
our families and our doctors and ourselves in consultation. The
Tsar decides and we must slavishly submit, accepting as much pain
as The TSOG ordains.

Can anybody think of more diamond-clear example of the basic
Fascist philosophy, or a more total logical contradiction of the U.S.
Constitution? Look back at the quote from Vico with which we
opened this oratorio: it may seem less "paranoid" now.

ANOTHER FAITH-BASED ORGANIZATION

I peeked at the G.O.P. convention a few times and concluded that we still live in the neurolinguistic Dark Ages.

Let me enlarge on that perhaps gnomic remark. I distinguish between **information**—all that humans can check by experience—as distinct from **noise**—those "things" (or non-things, or nothings) that they can only make noises or chatter about.

Examples: [A] I can say "If you open that box on the table, you will find exactly three chocolates inside." Going to the box and opening it, in the sensory-sensual continuum, will quickly confirm or refute my statement, because you will inevitably find [1] fewer than three chocolates, or perhaps none at all, [2] exactly three chocolates, or [3] more than three chocolates. Results [1] and [3] refute my statement; [2] confirms it.

But [B] I might also say "Opening God for similar investigation, you will find three persons inside," as in fact Romish Magick does say. No investigation of the sensory-sensual manifold can ever confirm or refute this. Scientific philosophers generally describe such statements (about things beyond conformation or refutation) as "meaningless." Following Korzybski, I call them "noise," and I venture that we cannot fathom our situation in space-time if we habitually confuse ourselves by mixing type [A] statements—information—with type [B] statements—noise. We may never achieve Total Clarity (short of infinity) but we should at least have the ability to distinguish between what humans can experience and what they can only blather about.

Distinguishing between these two types of statements seems necessary for sanity and survival, because all forms of illusion, delusion, mob hysteria, hallucination, etc.; dogma, bigotry, "madness," intolerance, etc.; "idealism," ideology, idiocy, obsession, etc. depend upon confusing them. The people who released

poison gas in the Tokyo subways, the Nazis, the Marxists, nut-cults
like Objectivism, CSICOP, Scientology, etc. represent some of the
horrors and curses unleashed by mixing Class [A] statements with
Class [B] statements.

I don't expect any better of the Democrats when their convention rolls around. Politics, like theology, consists of much noise
and NO information.

Force and Fire

Government is not reason, it is not eloquence, it is force;
like fire, a troublesome servant and a fearful master.
Never for a moment should it be left to irresponsible
action.

— George Washington

Kill a Kid for Christ

Lesley Stahl: "We have heard that half a million children
have died [in Iraq]. That's more children than died in
Hiroshima. And, you know, is the price worth it?"
Madeline Albright: "The price—we think the price is
worth it."

[Source: *60 Minutes*, 5/12/96]

Postscript: Clinton killed another half million before he left
office. The Republicans eagerly co-operated, but later recoiled in
moral outrage when they learned Bill also had blowjobs during
working hours.

You should WORK during working hours.

LYING BASTARD REVERSES HIMSELF AGAIN

There is no drug known to man which becomes safer when its production and distribution are handed over to criminals.

— Nick Davies

You know, it's a funny thing, every one of the bastards that are out for legalizing marijuana is Jewish. What the Christ is the matter with the Jews, Bob? What is the matter with them? I suppose it is because most of them are psychiatrists.

— Richard M. Nixon
[Source: http://www.washingtonpost.com]

CUDAHY, Calif. May 11, 2000—Vice President Bore today backed away from his earlier support of medical marijuana, saying he sees "no reliable evidence" that it is an effective pain reliever.

During a candidate forum in New Hampshire last December, Bore said that "where you have sufficient controls, I think that doctors ought to have that option."

But today, when asked by a student where he stood on a medical treatment that is legal in this state, Bore took a stronger stance against use of the drug.

"Right now, the science does not show me, or the experts whose judgment I trust, that it is the proper medication for pain and that there are not better alternatives available in every situation," he said in his usual toneless robot voice.

Bore's position on the issue has shifted several times and in some respects resembles the variety of comments he has made on the Elian Gonzalez case.

And that ain't the 'arf of it, dearie.

SWAMPY END OF THE GENE POOL

To enter life by way of the vagina is as good a way as
any.
— Henry Miller (1891–1980)

From a Darwinian perspective, Radical Feminism represents
the withdrawal of certain females from the breeding population.
This means that they will play no role in the future gene pool of
humanity. Considering the types who have taken this path—e.g.,
Steinem, Dworkin etc.—this appears a quite desirable eugenic
choice.

Now if only we could persuade the Radical Right to withdraw
from the future gene pool too, I would like the results even better.

Sooner or later we must take the bull by the tail and look
the facts in the face.
— Claude William Dunkenfield

MUNITIONS VS. MENTATIONS

The Gun Lobby says we need guns to protect ourselves from the present government. *Heiligefliegendekindersheisse!* Have they looked at the fuckin' government lately? To protect ourselves against the fuckin' current government, each citizen needs *at least* 1700 tactical nuclear weapons, at least 100 earth-to-air missiles, 50,000 flame throwers, 10,000 grenade launchers, and at least a hundred times as many assault weapons as the NRA now owns, plus biological and chemical (viral) weaponry.

Maybe instead of going to war with Washington, when they have us totally outgunned, we should try outsmarting the bastards?

GLAMIS HATH MURDERED SLEEP...
MACBETH SHALL SLEEP NO MORE

BERKELEY, Calif., July 9 (UPI)—Republicans have scarier and more frequent nightmares than Democrats, says one prominent dream researcher, Kelly Bulkeley, who teaches at the Graduate Theological Union in Berkeley, Calif.

"Half of the dreams of Republicans in my study were classified as nightmares, compared to only about 18 percent of the dreams of Democrats," Bulkeley reports.

[Source: http://www.vny.com/cf/
News/upidetail.cfm?QID=201006]

BENEFITS OF FAITH-BASED ORGANIZATIONS

More Lunacy

MAIDUGURI, Nigeria—More moronic Muslims burned down scores of hotels and bars in a northern Nigerian city in reaction to the lunar eclipse—which they blamed on fornicators.

Paramilitary police battled gangs of Muslim youths in the streets of Maiduguri for hours on Tuesday night.

Residents said at least 40 hotels or drinking houses were set ablaze. "The immoral acts committed in these places are responsible for this eclipse," police quoted one of the damned fools as saying.

[Source: Reuters]

Fair Thee Well, Titanic!

In Afghanistan, the Mashugginah Taliban have detained dozens of barbers for trimming the hair of young men in Kabul to look like Leonardo Di Caprio in the film *Titanic*.

> "We don't know for sure the precise number of the arrested people, but reportedly they exceed 30 and have been in the jail for over a week now for giving a Titanic hairstyle," said one barber, who wisely declined to be identified.

Maybe they're afraid of another eclipse?

Faith-Based Art Criticism, Yo Mama

A photography exhibit that includes a work depicting the late Redeemer of Biblical fame as a naked woman has stirred debate among the equally superstitious primitives in New York City. The work "Yo Mama's Last Supper" features the photographer, Renee Cox, nude and surrounded by 12 black apostles. It is part of an exhibit of 94 contemporary black photographers opening Friday at the Brooklyn Museum of Art.

Cox said the Last Supper image highlights legitimate criticisms of the church, including its refusal to ordain women as priests.

"Get over it!" she said. "Why can't a woman be Christ? We are the givers of life!"

"I think what they did is disgusting, it's outrageous," a local Mullah named Rudy Giuliani said. Other morons predict earthquakes or even eclipses.

[Source: http://www.cnn.com/2001/US/02/16/
museum.flap.ap/index.html]

Spellbound

A Ghanaian man was shot dead by a fellow villager while testing a magic spell designed to make him bulletproof.

Aleobiga Aberima, 23, and around 15 other idiots from Lambu village, northeast Ghana, had asked a Holy Man to make them invincible to bullets. After smearing his body with a concoction of herbs every day for two weeks, Aberima volunteered to be shot to check the spell had worked. The first bullet killed the stoopid bastid daid.

Well, at least he had Faith.

[Source: http://www.ireland.com/newspaper/
breaking/2001/0314/breaking59.htm]

LOGIC AND OTHER MALE PERVERSIONS

The revival of group hatreds in this country has dismayed and even frightened me ever since it began in the late 1960's.

Back in my high school and college days, in the late 1940's–early 1950's we all remembered Hitler very well, and only partly because he looked like Charlie Chaplin. Teachers taught us that Hitler was terrible, not because he hated the "wrong" group, but because hating any group is illogical, unscientific and leads ultimately to violence.

Groups are grammatical fictions; only individuals exist, and each individual is different.

Sometime while I was busy and didn't notice, Political Correctness took over Academia and they stopped teaching that. They started teaching that Hitler was terrible because he hated the wrong group, but it's okay to hate other groups.

Logic has nothing to do with it; logic itself has become suspect (just as happened in Nazi Germany).

This rebellion against rationality originally intended to make Radical Feminism and its doctrine of male fungibility respectable, and it succeeded, at least in the major media, but it also made fungible group hatred respectable in general. Now the anti-Semites and all the other hate mongers have begun crawling out from under their rocks, and Academia does not have the ammunition to argue against them. Academia cannot argue the rational principle that hatred of any group does not make sense; they dumped that when they dumped logic (as a "male" perversion).

The argument between Left and Right now consists only of debates about which groups we should hate.

I WALKED WITH A ZOMBIE

Guarde el vuelo del chupacabras!

Last night, a friend named Joe W. and I watched the first presidential debate on LSD, and we agreed that it seemed the funniest show of the new season. A Laff Riot! Four Stars!! Hodgepodge cluster!!!

Nor Dashed a Thousand Kim

We looked at a Three Stooges video before the Gush/Bore fiasco. While the magnomagnificent Stooges can't compare in sheer surrealism with Gush/Bore (two millionaires financed by billionaires, each claiming he wants to help us peasants) the Stooges' performances seemed more nuanced and "deeper", especially Moe's. We definitely need more of them. Their passing remains a great loss, especially Moe's.

$34,000,000+

As for the major clown show: We especially admired the skill of both Lying Bastards in managing to keep straight faces during the entire farce, while Joe and I were both "rolling in the aisles." We also admired the tact of Gush in not mentioning the fact that Bore had received more than $34,000,000 in bribes—er, I mean campaign financing—from the corporations that own the country.

But perhaps this tact derived from the fact that Gush had *also* received $34.000,000+ from the same corporations.[3]

GEORGE DON'T MAKE NO BULL MOVES

I suspeck that the guy wot sells those buttons that say "He's not a crackhead any more" should get prosecuted for false advertising; Gush seemed as speedy as a hair-trigger. Bore, meanwhile, seemed stoned out of his gourd, and a few times I thought he was about to announce that he only invented Internet on the 7th day, having spent the first six days creating the heavens and earth.

I wish the managers had given us a more meaningful debate—e.g., Gush claiming Donald Duck was funnier than Daffy Duck, and Bore defending Daffy—but still this remains the Laff Riot of the month.

French Canadian Bean Soup

Joe and I both thought Jim Lehrer also deserved special commendation for keeping a straight face, especially when looking directly into the camera and assuring us this "debate" concerned important issues.

GODDAM FLOATING WHOREHOUSE DEATH IS THE NAVIGATOR

In summary, it appeared to be a great election year if you kept well supplied with booze and hallucinogens.

DADA IS NOT DEAD WATCH YOUR OVERCOAT YOU KNUCKLEHEADS!

[3] See Jim Hightower's list on pages 68–69.

———————

I guess I'm Daffy Duck. I can dream about being Bugs
Bunny, but when I wake up I'm still Daffy Duck.

— Chuck Jones

———————

BENEFITS OF FAITH-BASED ORGANIZATIONS

Cults, Religions and B.S. in General

> Can we actually "know" the universe? My God, it's hard
> enough finding your way around in Chinatown.
>
> — Woody Allen

Last week, I happened to see two TV shows about "cults"—
"Scientology" and "Heaven's Gate" on A&E's Investigative
Reports—and they got me thinking. Each show had at least one
galoot claiming that the line between "cult" and "religion" seems
fuzzy at best, but each show also had a majority of folks who were
quite sure that could distinguish a "cult" from a "religion" by their
degree of "mind control" or "brainwashing." I think both groups
showed signs of neurolinguistic confusion.

I can only locate two clear-cut and empirical lines between a
"cult" and a "religion": [a] membership (voters) and [b] bank
account—[b] being a function of [a]. If a group has enough members to influence elections, it will also have a large bank account,
and these two factors will guarantee that the politicians, the cops
and the corporate media will treat it with respect, as a "religion."
With few members and little money, the same group could be
called a "cult" and treated accordingly, even to the extent of toast-
ing, roasting, frying, crisping and charbroiling, as happened to the
Branch Davidians in Waco.

This line remains obvious and visible to all observers; the only
problems arises when people try to draw a less "materialistic,"
more metaphysical, distinction between one gang of True Believers
and another. "Materialistic" questions about the sensory space-time
manifold can be answered—e.g., "Does that match-box have any

matches left in it?" Metaphysical questions about "mind control" or any other immeasurable "entity" or "essence" cannot be answered, and the best that can be said of them is that arguing about them has provided a certain amount of intellectual entertainment or verbal combat for a few thousand years, for those who enjoy that kind of pastime. Sort of like blindfold chess, you know.

I have no commitment to materialism as a philosophy which pretends to explain everything (which no correlation of words can ever do, and philosophy never seems more than a correlation of words to me). But, restricting myself to the scientific *method* of asking questions that have definite experiential answers, I observe no difference in operation between "cults" or "religions." Catholic nuns and priests vowing amoeboid asexuality seem no more or less weird than Heaven's Gate members who also make that choice. Mormon extraterrestrial cosmology seems as batshit crazy as Scientology, etc. Religions and cults all use the same techniques of brain damage, or "mind control"; i.e., they all instill *"faith based"* B.S.—Belief Systems.

Belief Systems contradict both science and ordinary "common sense." B.S. contradicts science, because it claims certitude and science can never achieve certitude: it can only say, "This model"—or theory, or interpretation of the data—"fits more of the facts known at this date than any rival model." We can never know if the model will fit the facts that might come to light in the next millennium or even in the next week.

> Outside of the killings, Washington has one of the lowest
> crime rates in the country.
> — Mayor Marion Barry, Washington, DC

But B.S. has an even more total incompatibility with what I loosely called "common sense." Except when we get dragged into a metaphysical, or Ideological, argument, we all know damn well how fallible we are. We know that our sense impressions can mislead us, for instance. If we see somebody who looks like Joe across the street, we are aware that it may be Joe or it may be some ginkus who looks a lot like Joe. We examine him empirically before classifying him quickly as Joe or not-Joe. We have learned that slow tentative judgments are safer than rapid certitudes.

After all, the Earth *looks* flat. Worse yet, if ten witnesses at an accident are questioned, ten slightly different stories always emerge—and sometimes the differences are huge, not slight.

——————

I have performed the following experiment in workshops for nearly 40 years now: I ask everybody in the class to describe the hall they passed through to get to the classroom. I must have tried this several hundred times and I have never encountered two people who agreed totally about what was or was not in the hall, the color of the walls, or any similar data. We do not walk through the "same" hall: we walk through a reality-tunnel constructed by our imprinted, conditioned, and learned brain-circuits.

The same experiment works with hearing, and other senses, as well as with vision and memory. Try it with a half-dozen friends. Let somebody with a watch say "Go!" and then all of you remain silent and listen for one full minute—60 surprisingly long seconds. You will all hear some sounds nobody else hears and miss some sounds everybody else caught.

Human brains are as individualized and unique as human fingerprints. We all live in different sensory universes, and nobody has a guarantee that his/her universe corresponds more exactly to the alleged "real universe" than anybody else's.

But if our perceptions are somewhat uncertain, then all of our ideas, which are deductions or inferences from perception, must also remain somewhat uncertain.

The late, sainted Dr. Timothy Leary used to put this in terms of a baseball metaphor: the best batters all had a lifetime batting average below .333. That means our greatest folk heroes missed the ball more than two out of three times they swung at it.

Now, maybe you have enough vanity to think you are more than twice as good at philosophy as Ted Williams was at baseball, but even then you'd only have an average around .600. To assume an average of 1.000 is to assert that you are a bit more than three times as smart with words as Babe Ruth was with baseballs—rather a conceited view, *nu* ?—and yet that's what every faith-based Belief System (B.S.) claims.

The function of religions and cults, including the political or Ideological ones, is to short-circuit the normal "common sense" process of doubt, investigation, further doubt, further investigation, further doubt, etc. The person with B.S. knows the "right answer" at all times and knows it *immediately.* This makes them very happy—and very annoying—because most of their "right answers" don't make sense to the rest of us.

Common sense and/or science require investigation and revision, etc. B.S. only requires a Rule Book (sacred scripture, *Das Kapital* or whatever) and a good *memory.*

People with "faith" represent mental health problem #1, because memorizing rule books cuts you off from sensory involvement with the existential world. It also produces the kind of intolerance that produces witch-hunts, Inquisitions, purges, Bushware 1.0, Bushware 2.0, etc.

Belief Systems, "faith," certitudes of all sorts, result from deliberately forgetting the fallibility of human brains, especially the brains of those who wrote your favorite rule book, and this leads to a paradoxical rejection of the best functions of the brain—namely, its ability to rethink, revise and correct itself. It also physically exhausts you, as Ezra Pound noted:

Awareness restful & fake is fatiguing
— Canto 85

If the world seems full and overstocked with stupid, crazy and half-asleep people, that is because it remains dominated by Belief Systems. Whether this B.S. operates under the label of religion or cult or Political Correctness, it shuts off all brain functions except memorization, and represents the strangulation of intelligence.

———

The most dangerous man to any government is the man who is able to think things out for himself, without regard to the prevailing superstitions and taboos. Almost inevitably he comes to the conclusion that the government he lives under is dishonest, insane, and intolerable.

— H.L. Mencken

———

ITHYPHALLIC IDOL

Now that his eight years in the White House have drawn to a close, I have begun to think of Slick Willy Clinton as the first really *entertaining* president in over 200 years. He makes all the others seem dull, and that will guarantee his immortality. As centuries turn into millennia, Bill will appear continually in all media, existing or not-yet-existing—e.g., drama, film, TV, Virtual Reality, you name it. All the best actors will want to play him, just as they now revel at the chance to play the randiest European royalty (Henry VIII, Charles II, Louis XVI—you know, *that* crowd). The best actresses will all play Monica Lewinski, who will achieve the archetypal status of Anne Boleyn, Nell Gwynn, Mme. Pompadour, etc. among the Fabulous Courtesans.

Eventually, my sense of cult and mythos tells me, Bill himself will surpass mere kings and join the legendary Roman emperors— Caligula, Tiberius, Commodus, et al.—or stand beside the bawdiest tales in the Finn Mac Cool cycle. Hell, give it 3000 years, and with the usual corrosions of time, archeologists will be found in violent dispute over whether certain ithyphallic statues represent Osiris, Priapus, or Our Own Bill; only carbon dating will settle these arguments.

Even today, Slick Willy appears as the star of a best-selling porn novel by Kenneth Starr, published and distributed by the Government Printing Office. He has eclipsed Errol Flynn as the symbol of raging male libido.

After all, who the hell remembers the actual politics of any of the sexual sociopaths of bygone ages just mentioned above? Henry VIII had six wives; that's what lives in folk memory. Nobody but professional historians knows or cares about his political positions.

Clinton will live in myth, legend, song and story as long as Nero. The folklore of humanity will never forget America's first president with a perpetual hard-on.

Thoughts to Ponder Again & Again & Again...

It depends on what the meaning of the word 'is' is. If the—if he—if 'is' means is and never has been, that is not—that is not the only one thing. It means there is none. That was a completely true statement.

— Bill Clinton, August 1998

BENEFITS OF FAITH-BASED ORGANIZATIONS

For Dr. Lecter's Scrapbook

What amateurs we all are, compared to Him.
— Hannibal Lecter, M.D.

A naked man wielding a Samurai sword tried to kill members of an English church congregation. Eden Strang, 26, left eleven churchgoers, including an elderly nun, seriously injured after attacking them with the sword and a knife.

Strang thought the other people in the church were demons.

He was only overcome after the Sunday morning worshippers at St. Andrew's Catholic Church, in Thornton Heath, London, whacked him on the head with a crucifix.

[Source: http://www.independent.ie/2000/153/w28a.shtml]

23 Countries?

VATICAN CITY—The Vatican acknowledged Tuesday a damning report that some priests and missionaries were forcing nuns to have sex with them, and were in some cases committing rape and forcing the victims to have abortions.

The Vatican said the issue was restricted to a certain geographical area, but the report cited cases in 23 countries.

[Source: Reuters]

CLINTON KILLS AGAIN

A few days before Bloomsday 2000 e.v. I lost another good friend. Peter McWilliams choked on his own vomit and died.

Peter, a cancer/AIDS patient, spent a lot of time vomiting before that final tragedy. Like many cancer patients, he found that TSOG chemotherapy caused that ugly side-effect, but, for a while, he found a solution. Marijuana banishes that kind of nausea and the voters of California voted to allow its use for such medical cases.

It seemed that Peter could spend his last months in relative peace, not puking his guts out every day.

He didn't know that the TSOG had junked the 10th Amendment along with the rest of the Constitution.[4]

When Bill Clinton officially announced the burial of the 10th Amendment and declared that neither the states nor the people had any medical rights anymore, all such power being reserved to the autocratic TSOG alone, Peter protested long and loud.

As a keynote speaker at the Libertarian National Convention 1998, Peter entertained attendees with his brilliant wit, but also defied and antagonized the TSOG. In a speech broadcast on C-Span, he called medical marijuana prohibition "an outrage within an outrage within an outrage." The first outrage, he said, to cheers, is the war on some drugs. The second outrage is the prohibition of what may be the least dangerous recreationally-used, drug, marijuana. And the third is that patients who need marijuana should be denied it, even arrested and sent to prison.

---

[4] The 10th Amendment states, "The powers not delegated to the United States by the Constitution, nor prohibited by it to the states, are reserved to the states respectively, or to the people."

It was less than three weeks later that federal prosecutors had Peter arrested and thrown in jail. In total violation of the Constitution and the will of the voters, the Court ordered him to stop using cannabis extracts and further ordered that the Piss Police check his urine regularly to ensure that he complied.

So Peter McWilliams went back to vomiting most of the day, every goddam day, until he choked on his puke and died.

You might want to visit Peter's very extensive web sites and see the legacy he left in books and much more:

http://www.petertrial.com
http://www.mcwilliams.com
http://www.marijuanamagazine.com

THE "CORRECT" DATE

Wait a Minute—
What Goddam Millennium?

I have used a variety of different calendars over the past 30 years—partly because I find it amusing to do so, but mostly for reasons of neurolinguistic self-education. (I employ a few dozen other devices of this sort to re-program myself out of conventional semantic grids: experiments, if you will, on Guinea Pig Bob.) For instance, I often use Ezra Pound's post-Christian calendar to date my musings. Beginning at midnight 30 October 1921 e.v.—when Joyce wrote the last words of *Ulysses*—this chronolog has six months for the phallic/solar divinities (Hepheistos, Zeus, Saturn, Hermes, Mars, Phoebus) and six for the vaginal/lunar divinities (Kupris, Juno, Athena, Hestia, Artemis, Demeter). In this system, I am writing these words on 8 Hestia 78 p.s.U.

Sometimes, I use the Discordian calendar, which dates everything from the Original Snub (see http://www.cs.cmu.edu/~tilt/principia/body.html) and makes today 1 Bureaucracy 3165 y.D.

As you can plainly see, we have 923 years to go until the next millennium (1001 p.s.U.) on the Poundian calendar, and 836 years to go to the next millennium (4001 y.D.) in the Discordian system.

A few other random calendars yield results like this:

Thelemic: present year 96——905 years until 1001 millennium.
Hebraic: present year 5759——242 years to 6001 millennium.
Mayan: present year 5113——888 years to 6001 millennium.
Pataphysical: present year 126——875 years to 1001 millennium.
Islamic: present year 1420——581 Islamic years (or 563 solar years) to 2001 millennium.

Why all the fuss, then, about the totally arbitrary Gregorian millennium? Well, maybe some intellectual Catholics (Jesuits, probably) have convinced themselves that Pope Gregory XIII created the "one true" calendar by tuning in—infallibly—to some Cosmic Clock. Einstein, however, has proven mathematically, and his successors have proven experimentally, that no such "one true" clock exists anywhere; and most of us don't believe in Papal infallibility, anyway. Dating the year after next (as I write this) 2001 (Gregorian) has as much and as little validity as dating it 5761 (Hebrew) or dating it 128 (Pataphysical). I think most people honest-to-Gawd believe the Papist date "is" the "real" date because they never stop to think about it.

I suspect, also, that most people do and say most of the things they do and say for exactly the same reason: **they never stop to think about it.** I know this sounds brutally cynical, but at least it explains the religious and political behaviors of our species, which otherwise seem totally beyond rational comprehension.

STOP AND THINK

War is just a racket... There are only two things we should fight for. One is the defense of our homes and the other is the Bill of Rights. War for any other reason is simply a racket.
— Major General Smedley Butler, USMC, twice awarded the Medal of Honor

Quo modo longe, Magna Cucurbita, quo modo longe?
— Eric Wagner

The New World Order

I think wrote Miss Bell to her mama
    that when not against the interests of Empire
we shd/ keep our pledges to the Arabs
        — Ezra Pound, Canto 52

CUBA URGES FREE ELECTIONS IN U.S.

Felipe Perez Roque, Cuba's foreign minister, said a new election in Florida would be a "reasonable" way to resolve the disputed vote for U.S. president and generously offered to send Cuban observers to ensure fair balloting.

I guess he thought a great many of us wanted a free election. Only a few really cared a hoot, it now appears.

Roque also questioned whether in future U.S. votes, "it would be necessary to have a more rigorous or strict international scrutiny regarding the transparency of elections."

[Source: *Associated Press* November 10, 2000 e.v.]

———⇒●⇐———

The only book you've got to read is *The Godfather*.
That's the only one that tells how the world is really run.
— Roberto Calvi, President, Banco Ambrosiano;
stretched, London, 18/6/1982

———⇒●⇐———

THE WRONG GUY: PART I

Several news organizations have evaluated the disputed ballots in the state of Florida to determine who might have actually won the vote in the state if a hand recount had not been halted by the TSOG Supreme Court.

But John Gibson of Fox News Channel (12/15/00) would rather not know what really happened in Florida: "Is this a case where knowing the facts actually would be worse than not knowing? I mean, should we burn those ballots, preserve them in amber, or shred them?"

Gibson added: "George Bush is going to be president. And who needs to know that **he's not a legitimate president?** Al Gore? Jesse Jackson? His political opponents? How does it do any good for the country to find out that, by somebody's count, **the wrong guy is president?"**

[Source: FAIR-L Fairness & Accuracy in Reporting Media analysis, critiques and news reports December 20, 2000 e.v.]

———◆———

I do not feel obliged to believe that the same God who has endowed us with sense, reason, and intellect has intended us to forgo their use.

— Galileo Galilei

———◆———

The higher of them, the more jackass.
— Bartolomeo Vanzetti

———><•<———

Police Find Locked Ballot Box at Miami Hotel

MIAMI (Reuters)—Miami police on Friday found a locked ballot box from the disputed Florida election at a downtown hotel, a police officer said on Saturday.

Police Lt. Diego Ochoa, a 26-year veteran of the police department, said he came forward with the consent of his commanding officer and arrangements were now underway for election officials to pick up the box.

The TSOG's sure going to need a lot of **faith-based organizations...**

———><•<———

God bless George W. Bush and the United States of America.
— Al Gore, concession speech

———><•<———

Although we may never know with complete certainty the identity of the winner of this year's presidential election, the identity of the loser is perfectly clear. It is the nation's confidence in the judge as an impartial guardian of law.
— Justice John Paul Stephens

———><•<———

Is this a pubic hair in my coke?
— Justice Clarence Thomas (attributed)

DAFFY DUCK FOR PRESIDENT

I just caught some local news and wotdoyaknow? Santa Cruz county, where I live, has its own lost/found ballot scandal—of a peculiarly Santa Cruzian sort.

It seems somebody found 300+ uncounted ballots. Explanation by the election officials: all these ballots contained bizarre write-in candidates, marked in "unconventional" ways. Nonetheless, with fraud charges flying everywhich way, the officials are plowing through them to make sure no ballots for "real" "serious" candidates (like Gush or Bore) got in the shitpile by mistake.

I wonder what bizarre names got written in... Dracula? Wile E. Coyote? Cthulhu? Jerry Garcia? Francis the Talking Mule? John Hinkley? Ubu Roi? Pancho Villa? Lamont Cranston? Pontius Pilate? Hannibal Lecter?

And what "unconventional" markings? The best I can think of—just use a dayglo marker to scrawl

NOBODY

in huge letters across the whole card...

My gawd, maybe some of my neighbors are even weirder than me?

With Justice for Whom?

The courts apply all criminal laws in this nation in a mild, rational and humane manner...if the defendant is rich.

———⟫•⟨———

In individuals, insanity is rare; but in groups, parties, nations and epochs, it is the rule.

— Friedrich Nietzsche

———⟫•⟨———

Nobody Won!?!

for Col. Hugh Romney, USAF (ret.)

I have never enjoyed an election more, or had my animal spirits raised higher by the results. I feel, in short, just like I did in Berlin the week before the Wall came down: a quantum jump seems about to happen.

My perennial candidate, Nobody, scored another stunning victory. **The majority of citizens simply ignored the Gush/Bore/ TSOG Control Machine, and "voted for Nobody": i.e., didn't vote at all.** Unlike alienated artists of the past, I belong to the *majority* party—the millions who looked over the candidates and decided they trusted Nobody.

According to the latest (wobbly) figures, since Gush and Bore each got the vote of (roughly) 25% of the eligible voters, and Nobody got the vote of (roughly) 50%, then Nobody won. Adding the "protest votes" for Nader, Browne, Buchanan etc., Nobody won even bigger, around 55% since, in this carefully rigged system, third party votes are, in effect, votes for Nobody. The people who voted for those "minority" candidates certainly didn't expect them to win; they just expressed their contempt for the Two Lying Bastards more actively than those of us who just stayed home, got stoned and looked at Three Stooges videos.

I celebrate the majority with Whitmanesque rhapsody. The so-called Elite—specifically, the 1/2 of 1% who own damn near everything, especially the politicians and the media—spent

THREE BILLION DOLLARS on this malign fiesta and still couldn't convince most of us that a choice between two over-rouged old whores like Gush and Bore matters a damn.

This seems wonderful to me. Liberty can survive only as long as most people distrust their government, and falls into decline and the "sickness unto death " whenever the people trust a government too damn much.

Besides, I think it's time to abolish politicians entirely and let everybody participate in self-government via Internet. We needed "representatives" in the 18th Century because we couldn't all go to Washington. Meanwhile, times changed and our "representatives" have sold us out to the corporations, as we in the majority party all agree, whatever our differences in other matters. And we don't need "representatives" anymore; we have the Net technology to represent ourselves.[5]

In that (r)evolutionary sense, every vote for Nobody really represents a vote for Everybody.

How Government Operates

The Florida ballot fiasco has produced at least one valuable benefit: It has shown us exactly how government actually operates.

— Harry Browne, Libertarian Presidential candidate, at
http://www.worldnetdaily.com/
pageOneCommentary.shtml

Fornication—at least that is something good. What else is there to do? Fornicate and take drugs against the terrible strain of idiots who govern the world.

— Albert Szent-Gyorgyi, Nobel Laureate in Medicine and Physiology, *The New York Times*, Feb. 20, 1970

---

[5] I develop this idea further in *The Tale of the Tribe* (New Falcon Publications.)

THE WRONG GUY: PART II

Two newly published studies of the ballots cast in the 2000 U.S. presidential election confirm that Democrat Al Gore was the choice of more Florida voters than Republican George W. Bush, who was installed as president after an unprecedented intervention by the TSOG's Supreme Court.

One study was conducted by the *Washington Post*, the other by Tribune Co., which owns the *Chicago Tribune*, the *Orlando Sentinel*, and the *Fort Lauderdale Sun-Sentinel*. The analysis found that of the more than 60,000 ballots in the eight counties showing overvotes—the bulk of the statewide total—Gore's name was marked on 46,000, while Bush was marked on only 17,000. **This includes several thousand ballots in which both Gore and Bush were marked.**

The notorious "butterfly ballot" in Palm Beach County accounted for 8,000 of the Gore overvotes, most of them double votes for Gore and far-right Reform Party candidate Patrick Buchanan, who was listed across from Gore on the ballot, with his punch-hole close to the names of Gore and Lieberman. Gore-Buchanan voters in Palm Beach County voted 10–1 Democratic in the U.S. Senate race.

[Source: *EcoNews* http://www.ecologynews.com/Prague
http://mujweb.cz/www/ecologynews/]

———

God bless George W. Bush and the United States of America.

— Al Gore, concession speech

BENEFITS OF FAITH-BASED ORGANIZATIONS

Kwik-Kleen Kult

TV star Courteney Cox has joined an innovative church that claims to "clean" souls simply by taking their photograph.

The actress believes she can achieve "energetic balancing" by storing her picture for up to a year in a special machine at the Energetic Matrix Church of Consciousness.

[Source: http://www.the-sun.co.uk]

Fear in the Night

A businessman has confessed to sending 'orrible spooks & ghouls & ghosts to attack schoolgirls in eastern Kenya. The businessman (unnamed) was arrested over the weekend after the pupils of Itokela Girls Secondary School marched to the district commissioner's office to protest against an invasion of ghosts at the school, the *East African Standard* said.

The girls claimed the culprit had hired the ghosts to torment them after his daughter left the school.

The businessman apparently agreed to meet the cost of exorcising the spirits, but the story does not specify which faith-based organization will get the contract.

[Reuters, Monday June 5, 2001 cited in http://www.blather.net]

Unidentified Flying Virgin

Cairo, Egypt—Every Monday night Marcelle Maurice comes to Saint Mark's Church to see the Blessed Virgin Mary flutter by. Marcelle says the BVM usually has "flashing lights" (UFOs?)

accompanying her, and "big white doves" as well. "Thousands" of Christians have flocked to the Church to watch for the flying Virgin, but Moslems say they can't see her.

[Source: http://abcnews.go.com/sections/
world/DailyNews/virgin000911.html]

———➤●◄———

Meanwhile, we must all face the fact
that our leaders are certifiably insane
or worse.

— William S. Burroughs, *Last Words*

———➤●◄———

IDEAS TO REMEMBER

Every jury in the land is tampered with and falsely instructed by the judge when it is told that it must accept as the law that which has been given to them, or that they can decide only the facts of the case.
— Lord Denham, O'Connell v Rex (1884)

The jury has the power to bring in a verdict in the teeth of both the law and the facts.[6]
— Supreme Court Justice Oliver Wendell Holmes, Jr.
Homing v District of Columbia, 138 (1920)

If a juror accepts as the law that which the judge states, then that juror has accepted the exercize of absolute authority of a government employee and has surrendered a power and a right that once was the citizen's safeguard of liberty.
— Bancroft, *History of the Constitution*

It is not only the juror's right, but his duty, to find the verdict according to his own best understanding, judgment and conscience, though in direct opposition to the directions of the court.
— John Adams

---

[6] That is, the jury—not the judge—is the final arbiter of both the facts *and* the law. Thus, if a jury believes that a law is unjust (either in general or in a particular case), it may find the defendent not guilty, despite the law (and despite judicial instructions to the contrary). This doctrine is known as "Jury Nullification." For more information, refer to The Fully Informed Jury Association (http://www.fija.org). [Ed.]

—»•«—

If the jury feels the law is unjust, we recognize the undisputed power of the jury to acquit, even if its verdict is contrary to the law as given by a judge, and contrary to the evidence.
— 4th Circuit Court of Appeals, U.S. v Moylan, 1969

—»•«—

When a jury acquits a defendant even though he or she clearly appears to be guilty, the acquittal conveys significant information about community attitudes and provides a guideline for future prosecutorial discretion... Because of the high acquittal rate in prohibition cases in the 1920's and early 1930's, prohibition laws could not be enforced. The repeal of these laws is traceable to the refusal of juries to convict those accused of alcohol traffic.

— Sheflin and Van Dyke,
Law and Contemporary Problems,
43, No. 4, 1980

DADDY, WHAT DOES
"CORPORATE MEDIA" MEAN?

An estimated 80% of all news outlets in the United States are now corporate owned, according to a recent survey.

A few corporations decide what news we see and why, and it decides to an alarming extent what movies, books, and television programs will be pushed at the public, and which will get buried in the back yard with the kitty litter.

Even scarier, these TSOGlomerates are immune from any anti-trust controls. In 1969, when bigger newspapers first started buying up smaller newspapers, the Supreme Court opposed these activities, saying that although freedom to publish is a Constitutional right, freedom to buy up other publishers to silence them is not a right. However, we have a new TSOG-style Supreme Court now...

Who Owns What?

CNN: owned by Time Warner/AOL, which now controls a major share of the online market, including the increasingly well-read AOL news, and owns Turner Network, numerous theme parks, sports teams, retail stores and publishing companies, Book-of-the Month Club, Time Magazine, Fortune magazine, Compu-Serve, and Netscape; and holds major interests in Wal-Mart and Bell Atlantic, along with significant interests in Gateway, Hughes Electronics and SBC Communications.

ABC: Owned by Disney, which also owns 10 television stations, 44 radio stations, and 219 affiliated TV stations, various publishing and recording companies, and movie studios.

CBS: Owned by Viacom, which owns at least three dozen television stations, 200 affiliated stations, 160 radio stations, the Blockbuster movie rental chain, Simon & Schuster publishing, and King World Features.

FOX: Owned by Rupert Murdoch's News Corporation, which owns 22 television stations in the U.S. and 159 affiliated stations, along with *The New York Post* and *The Weekly Standard*, various satellite systems, book publishing concerns, and at least 130 newspapers overseas.

NBC: owned by General Electric, which also owns CNBC jointly with Dow Jones, and MSNBC jointly with Microsoft. GE also owns several financial services, insurance companies, and of course, is one of the world's leading techno companies, producing everything from light bulbs to nuclear equipment.

Traditionally, GE has been one of the biggest defense contractors ever, with keen financial interest in the TSOG program of Perpetual War, and has its finger in many pies, including ***Enron.***

[Source: http://www.democrats.com/view.cfm?id=127]

WORDS TO PONDER AGAIN AND AGAIN

Never before in all history have the inequities and the momentums of unthinking money-power been more glaringly evident to so vastly large a number of now literate, competent, and constructively thinking all-around-the-world humans. There's a soon-to-occur critical-mass moment when the intuition of the responsibly inspired majority of humanity, in contradistinction to the angered Luddites and avenging Robin Hoods, faced with comprehensive functional discontinuity of nationally contained techno-economic system, will call for and accomplish a world-around reorientation of our planetary affairs.

> — R. Buckminster Fuller,
> "Can't Fool Cosmic Computer"
> *Grunch of Giants* (St. Martin's Press, 1983), p. 89

God bless George W. Bush and the United States of America.

> — Al Gore, concession speech

LAS DIE LASAGNE WEITER FLIEGEN!

The European Union has angered the Bush administration by taking America to task for ignoring "human rights norms" in its refusal to abolish ancient druidic rites of human sacrifice.

Washington's irritation was compounded when, in December, a clause was inserted in the EU charter of fundamental rights stating that no prisoner could be extradited to a country that had the death penalty.

[Source: EcoNews http://www.ecologynews.com/Prague
http://mujweb.cz/www/ecologynews]

Postscript 1

About 100+ years ago, Frazer pointed out in *The Golden Bough* that human sacrifice depends on the logic of "We've always had human sacrifice and the crops have been good. If we stop human sacrifice, the crops might fail and we'll all starve." He commented ironically that many Englishmen still think that way... Well, the English have advanced in 100 years, but Americans largely haven't.

Postscript 2

Ten American states—20% of the whole—have abolished human sacrifice.

Civilization remains *possible*.

> LAWSUIT: A machine which you go into as a pig and come out as a sausage.
> — Ambrose Bierce

BENEFITS OF FAITH-BASED ORGANIZATIONS

Church and Cancer

Consumer groups and politicians in Rome have charged that the likely cause of a cancer cluster around the Vatican is a high-powered radio transmission tower used by the Church to spread the Church's propaganda. Some Romans call it "Vatican Smog."

[Source: http://www.blather.net]

Night Music

There ought to be limits to freedom!
— George W Bush, May 21, 1999
http://www.gwbush.com

If this were a dictatorship, it'd be a heck of a lot easier, just so
long
as
I'm the dictator.
— George W Bush, CNN transcript 12/18/2000

BUGS BUNNY AND OTHER UFO VICTIMS

Although few people remember this, Bugs Bunny was the first UFO "abductee" in a 1952 cartoon called "Hasty Hare."

The next case did not occur until nine years later, in 1961, when the famous Betty and Barney Hill encountered the "Greys" from Zeta Reticuli, who molested them sexually and otherwise, and were also wearing Nazi uniforms. At least, Barney Hill remembered the malign midgets as garbed in Nazi regalia; Betty, for some odd reason never did recall that poignantly puzzling detail.

Now "many millions" have suffered the same sort of "extraterrestrial" sexual abuse, according to Abductees Anonymous, a support group for survivors. Budd Hopkins has become as famous as a rock star, for helping people "remember" such experiences. And this is not just another New Age fad. Dr. John Mack, a distinguished scientist on the staff of the psychiatry department of Harvard University has written two books on the subject; and Harvard, which once gave Dr. Timothy Leary the bum's rush for having weird ideas, allows Dr. Mack to remain on their staff, with all the prestige that bestows upon this eldritch and Lovecraftian topic.

Dr. Mack seems like a sane and sensible man, by the way (I've met him) and he frankly admits that he's not quite sure what kind of "reality" these experiences occur in, except that it sure ain't consensus reality—but something more like the non-ordinary reality of Carlos Castaneda's Don Juan books, or of the mystics of all traditions...or of Tim Leary and his merry band of acid astronauts.

Peculiarly, both law enforcement and mainstream science seem to have no interest in this matter at all, at all.

I find that startling. Imagine what would happen if "many millions" of U.S. citizens said they had been **sexually assaulted by**

aliens from Afghanistan or Iraq, instead of aliens from Outer Space. Obviously, there would be no scientific tabu against investigating such cases, and Congress might even have declared war on the invaders by now. If the subjects claimed, as most of Dr. Mack's subjects do claim, that they now love their kidnappers and have learned from them important ecological warnings and other sermons about how wicked and wretched our society is, this would be considered evidence that they had been "brainwashed" as well as raped ("Stockholm Syndrome"). This difference in scientific and political reactions to atrocities by human aliens and nonhuman aliens seems even more confusing than the rest of this mystery.

Bill Cooper, who claims to be a former Naval Intelligence officer, alleges that he saw papers revealing a treaty between our government and the "Greys," who are providing our military with advanced technology. The little inhuman bastards have broken the treaty, Cooper says, not only by sexual and/or genetic meddling with our citizens, but also by mutilating a lot of cattle, yet our government can't stop them because of their superior weapons. The Outer Space monsters were also behind the assassination of John F. Kennedy, he says.

Dr. Mack, on the other hand, is no longer sure what kind of "reality" we are dealing with here, as noted, and even seems unclear about the literalness of the abductions. In his second book, *Passport to the Cosmos* (Crown Publishers, New York, 1999) he no longer calls his subjects "abductees" but instead "experiencers," although he remains convinced that they experienced *something* and that the experience is real in *some* sense.

Consider, in this context, the investigations of Dr. Cory Hammond of the University of Utah, former president of the American Society of Clinical Hypnosis. Dr. Hammond has had a lot of clients who, under hypnosis, "remember" hideous incidents of Satanic rituals, infant sacrifice, sado-masochism, coprophilia and assorted horrors. Dr. Hammond believes that these cases, and the data he has unearthed on the Satanic cult in general, prove that three distinct groups working together—Nazis, the C.I.A. and NASA— have been secretly and brutally programming American children for over 50 years to make them part of "a Satanic order that will rule the world."

Can we believe both Dr. Mack and Dr. Hammond at the same time, and accept that while extraterrestrials or even weirder non-humans have been raping people and teaching ecology, another conspiracy is simultaneously torturing and abusing children to make them Slaves of Satan? Or might we more economically assume that a lot of people have had a lot of nonordinary experiences—psychedelic trips without drugs—and that we all tend to interpret these Wig Outs according to our own hopes and fears?

Or, consider the model offered by Dr. Jacques Vallee, who has been investigating UFOs for more than 30 years. Dr. Vallee has suggested as one *possible* explanation, a vast experiment in mind control and behavior mod by some Intelligence Agency (he doesn't try to guess *which* one...). Could both Dr. Mack's cases and Dr. Hammond's cases represent persons who fell victim to this and retain only shattered and distorted memories of their ordeal? Considering what has already leaked about the CIA's MK-ULTRA research, this hypothesis does not seem altogether extravagant.

Bill Cooper, the guy who says the Greys were behind the JFK hit, has also considered a variation on Vallee's theory. He himself, Cooper says, may have been deceived by his superiors in Naval Intelligence. But in that case, he points out, the government (I no longer feel safe in calling it "our government") must be using the Grey mythology as a cover-up to hide something else—something even worse than selling us out to rapists from Reticuli.

Frankly, I cannot accept either the blind faith of the True Believers or the dogmatic denials of the Establishment. Like Dr. Mack, I think the whole topic needs less sensationalism and more open-minded research.

After all, the next person engulfed by this non-ordinary reality might be you or me. Especially if we dare to criticize the C.I.A....or even Bushware 2.0...

MERE FACTUAL INNOCENCE

Mere factual innocence is no reason not to carry out a death sentence properly reached.
— U.S. Supreme Court Justice Antonin Scalia

Evidence of innocence is irrelevant.
— Virginia Attorney General Mary Sue Terry

Entertaining claims of actual innocence would have...[a] very disruptive effect...on the need for finality in death penalty cases.
— U.S. Supreme Court Chief Justice William Rehnquist

The execution of a person who can show that he is innocent comes perilously close [!?!?] to simple murder.
— U.S. Supreme Court Justice Harry Blackman

THE MASKS OF REALITY

In the dialectic between nature and the socially constructed world, the human organism is transformed. In
this dialectic man produces reality and thereby produces
himself.
— Berger & Luckman, *The Social Creation of Reality*

Would you believe that an English football star has stolen the
infant Jesus—four times, from four different Italian churches—and
is holding him or them for a ransom of 100,000,000 lire?

Well, neither would I, but it seems to have happened, sort of.
But then most things in this confusing modern world only seem to
have happened...sort of...like the (s)election of Bushware 2.0... I
mean, like, ever since they gave the Nobel Peace Prize to Henry
Kissinger, and openly placed a Tsar where the Constitution used to
stand, it seems impossible to distinguish "reality" from satire, or
even from surrealism. (Readers of this book must have noticed that
already...)

Luther Blissett, to start at the top, was once the best footballer
in England, as well known and beloved as O.J. Simpson was over
here, before he got a reputation for cutting throats. Now Mr.
Blissett is a coach in Watford, UK. Unlike O.J., he has never been
charged with a major felony, or even with jay-walking. He says he
knows nothing about the *other* Luther Blissett who, in addition to
holding Jesus for ransom, has written a number of anarchist tracts,
including a left-wing history of the Renaissance, and is suspected
by the Italian authorities of being a group rather than a person.

Some, of course, claim he is the Devil.

It seems to have begun—the miraculous multiplication of Blissetts—when the true, original Luther Blissett became a hero, and a controversial figure in Milan while playing football there ten years ago.

Luther Blissett the Second, and the Third, Fourth and Fifth, manifested a few years later when four workers were arrested for riding on a train without a ticket. Each insisted his name was "Luther Blissett," and stuck to that name, even when hauled into court for sentencing.

Then other Luther Blissetts began to appear, on Internet and even in bookstores. As to whether he or they were or are a group or an individual, they or he (or she) offered the following explication:

> Luther Blissett is not a "teamwork identity" as reported by the journalists; rather, it is a multiple single. The "Luther Blissetts" don't exist, only Luther Blissett exists. Today we can infuse ourselves with vitality by exploring any possibility of escaping conventional identities... The struggle is still against the language of the powers-that-be.

If that isn't perfectly clear to non-anarchists, recall the Dada movement in Switzerland during World War I. The Dadaists, in total rebellion against the insanity of war and the general insanity of everything else, held poetry readings at which the poet was drowned out by other Dadaists with noise-makers. They had art exhibits where the audience were provided with axes at the door and told to destroy any paintings they didn't like. They held lectures in public urinals. In short, they began the "post-modern" revolution against conventional "identities" and the language that divides things and people into classes.

In 1923, in Paris, the Surrealists held their first art show. To enter the gallery, the audience had to pass through a garden with an incongruous taxi standing in the way. Working their way around the cab, they had the opportunity to observe that it was raining inside of it but not outside. (A whimsy of Salvador Dali.) Once into the gallery, the audience, or the victims—as you prefer—confronted a sign devised by Andre Breton:

DADA IS NOT DEAD!
WATCH YOUR OVERCOAT!

Or, to move closer to the present enigma, consider the time that novelist Ken Kesey met novelist Terry Southern. Kesey found to his delight that Southern seemed just as funny in person as he was in his books and they had a wonderful time together. Only long after did Kesey discover that he had not met Terry Southern at all. He had met somebody else—an "imposter" in pre-anarchist language.

I also met Terry Southern once, or think I did, and also found him hilarious. Of course, with Kesey's experience in mind, I might wonder if I actually met the "real" Terry Southern. But modern anarchists would inform me that even asking such a question is buying into the language and metaphysics of the ruling class which oppresses us by defining us. One can only say that Terry Southern has become a multiple single.

———

Anyway, once Luther Blissett was firmly established as both an individual sports hero in England and one or many anarcho-surrealists in Italy, life became more interesting for Europeans—the way it was for most of us on this side of the pond in the 1980's when we could watch Ronald Reagan play the hero's buddy in a morning college football movie on TV, then catch him again playing the hero himself in a Western in the afternoon, and finally see him a third time playing the President on the evening news.

The Italian Luther Blissett(s) then published a book of essays allegedly by the Arab-American anarchist, Hakim Bey.[7] It later

---

[7] Bey himself has not added any clarity by spreading conflicting rumors that he was previously court-poet to a Maharajah in India, librarian to the late Shah of

turned out that only one essay was by Bey;the rest were forgeries—although one was a translation from John Zerzan, the Oregon anarchist who became famous, or infamous, for declaring that the Unabomber was his personal hero.

Things became a bit stranger when the infant Jesus disappeared from a church in Belvedere, followed quickly by the vanishings of three more infant Jesi from churches in Marittimo, Tortora and Diamante, all four cities being on the Tyrrhenian coast.

"What is the Buddha?" a student once asked a Zen Master.
"The one in the hall," replied the Master.
"But the one in the hall is a statue, a piece of *wood*!"
"True..."
"Then what is the Buddha?"
"The one in the hall."

Italians seem to understand Zen logic better than most Europeans[8] and the dematerializing Jesi (or Jesuses?) really caused mass emotional reactions. It was as if Andy Warhol had sued Campbell Soup for selling cheap imitation Warhols.

Then the ecclesiastical authorities received a communiqué (written on an old Olivetti typewriter) demanding that the Church distribute one hundred million lire to the poor—or else:

> The Holy Child will be destroyed. Anyway, you only
> care for the money, not for the Child's sacral value... In

Iran, a Taliban terrorist, leader of the Sufi order, the reincarnation of Judy Garland, etc.

[8] Except the Irish; See "Is the Face on Mars Moishe Horwitz?: The Ethnomethodology of NASA Press Releases as Mythic Narrative," Timothy F.X. Finnegan, *Journal of the Royal Sir Myles na gCopaleen Theo-Chemical Institute* VII, 473.

Calabria people die of hunger, thirst, unemployment, mafia, corruption and usury. Illegal employment is the rule.
There are no houses. The Church doesn't care and gets richer. If you don't distribute a 100 million lire worth of food...the Holy Child will be smashed into pieces.

— Luther Blissett

The prototype Luther Blissett in England told the press he didn't understand what was going on. "They keep doing all sorts of things and I keep getting the credit or the blame for it."

The police in Italy announced that they suspected a sort of Luther Blissett-X—not the "original" multiple singularity of anarchist pranksters, but a band of professional art thieves *masquerading as the masqueraders*. The infants stolen have a high commercial value, said the suspicious cops, and instead of being smashed they may be sold to the highest bidders like the famous Maltese Falcon.

One incautious priest, in Belvedere, remarked worriedly that the only way to prevent future thefts would be to lock all the churches and keep everybody out. The press gleefully quoted him. If there were no godless anarchists thinking of that before, there certainly are now...

You can follow future developments through the following websites:

http://www.syntac.net/lutherblissett
http://www.LutherBlissett.net
http://www.geocities.com/Paris/Leftbank/6815
http://news.bbc.co.uk/hi/english/sport/football/newsid_293
    000/293678.stm

———➤●◀———

I sort of think I know how the first Luther Blissett feels, because a lot of people on Internet still claim I was murdered by the C.I.A. on 22 February 1994. No denials by me have stopped this absurd & abominable rumor, because the conspiracy buffs who believe it also believe that the C.I.A. replaced me with an "android" or humanoid robot which writes and talks just like "Robert Anton Wilson." Some even claim that my evident "sincerity" in claiming I am "Robert Anton Wilson" just proves how advanced the secret technology of the C.I.A. is: any really good RAW android would not only write, talk and look like me, but would necessarily think it "was" me...

As Oscar Wilde said, "The reality of metaphysics is the reality of masks."

The Accordian Man

Records indicate that the Oswald who enlisted in the Marines was 5´11˝. Comrade Oswald, who went to Russia, was 5´6˝. while the dead version measured in at 5´9˝.

— Richard Belzer, *UFOs, JFK and Elvis*

BENEFITS OF FAITH-BASED ORGANIZATIONS

Rockford Files

A Roman Catholic priest smashed his car into a Rockford, Illinois abortion clinic recently, then chopped at the building with an axe until the owner fired two shotgun blasts to stop him, police said.

The clinic was not open and nobody was injured in the attack. The priest drove through a door at the Abortion Access Northern Illinois Women's Center about 8:15 a.m. EDT. He was swinging an axe when the clinic's owner fired a 12-gauge shotgun twice. He did not hit the deranged Holy Man, Rev. John Earl, 32, who was arrested and charged with burglary and felony criminal damage to property. Earl was being held in lieu of $10,000 bail.

[Source: *Associated Press* Saturday, 30 September 2000 15:18:26–0700 (PDT)]

"Supreme Truth"

A key member of Japan's doomsday cult, dubbed a "murder machine" by the media for his crimes, including taking part in the deadly 1995 gas attack on the Tokyo subway, was sentenced to death yesterday.

Tokyo District Court Judge Kiyoshi Kimura said former Aum Shinri Kyo ("Supreme Truth") cult member, Yasuo Hayashi, 42,, deserved the sentence because he released the largest amount of poisonous sarin gas in the attack, which claimed 12 lives and injured thousands.

Prosecutors charged that Hayashi was directly responsible for the deaths of eight people by carrying three plastic bags of the deadly gas on to a packed commuter train. He released the gas by puncturing the bags with the sharpened tip of an umbrella.

Hayashi is was the second cult member to receive the death penalty. The other, Masato Yokoyama, has appealed. Hayashi's lawyers were quoted as saying they would seek an appeal.

"This morning I prayed that he would get the death penalty. I am satisfied," a parent of one of his victims said after the ruling.

[Source: http://www.blather.net]

Christian Love

BELFAST, Northern Ireland (AP)—Police came under attack from both Protestants and Catholics early Tuesday, in rioting prompted by an ugly confrontation that terrified girls on their first day of classes at a Roman Catholic elementary school.

Schoolgirls cowered and clung to their parents on the first day of classes Monday while angry Protestant demonstrators tried to block the building's entrance.

Police with clubs, shields and attack dogs drove the protesters back from Holy Cross Primary School, which lies in a Protestant enclave of this bitterly divided city.

Most of the girls—among them 4- and 5-year-olds attending their first day of school in new red uniforms—were sent home early, many in tears. A fleet of Catholic-run black taxis ferried them past lines of police in helmets and shields, while many Protestants shouted curses and insults.

One Catholic parent compared the scene to school integration battles in the United States.

"This looks like Alabama in the 1960's," said Brendan Mailey, leader of a Catholic parents group that insisted on using the front door of the school, which is in the small Protestant section of Ardoyne, a mostly Catholic area.

The conflict prompted widespread violence after dark, as rival mobs of Protestant and Catholic lunatics attacked police and homes in north Belfast.

9-1-1
EMERGENCY

Somebody blew hell out of the center of International Capitalism (WTC) and its Company Cop (the Pentagon), but Bushware 2,0 and the corporate media call it an attack on "freedom."

And a bomb at the nearest Ho House would get called an attack on "chastity"?

War Against Some Terrorists:
7 Ways of Looking at a Monkey-House

I

Just as the War Against Drugs would make some kind of sense if they honestly called it a War Against Some Drugs, I regard Dubya's current Kampf as a War Against Some Terrorists. I may remain wed to that horrid heresy until he bombs C.I.A. headquarters in Langley, VA.

II

I turned on CNN a few days ago and a White House robot announced that the rebels in Chechnya "were" no longer freedom fighters but "are" now terrorists with "clear" links to Osama bin Laden.

CNN provided no details about whether the transformation occurred in a sudden miraculous flash like the transubstantiation of the host in a Catholic mass, or happened slowly and gradually like Darwinian evolution.

In a related bulletin, Russia pledged its support in the War
Against Some Terrorists, and will presumably start with those
bastards in Chechnya.

III

DO *NOT* ADJUST YOUR MIND:
IT IS
REALITY
THAT IS MALFUNCTIONING

IV

The plight of Bill Maher reminds me of something Ezra Pound
wrote about London in 1919: "A single intelligent remark can
destroy a man's entire career."

V

A friend in Israel just sent me an email quoting George Bush
saying we should all go to Disneyland. It didn't surprise me. I kind
of suspect George lives in Disneyland all the time, with Mickey
and Goofy and Osama bin Laden and all the "faith-based
organizations" in the world.

VI

As Voltaire said, "The only way to comprehend what mathe-
maticians mean by Infinity is to contemplate the extent of human
stupidity."

VII

Pfui!

PEARL HARBOR REDUX?

What happened on Flight 11—and whodunit?

When placing the cell phone call to her ground manager, Sweeney stated that were **four** hijackers on flight 11, and confirmed that their seat numbers were in rows **9 and 10**.

The FAA memo also identified a passenger in seat 10B who, it was claimed, shot another passenger in seat 9B.

The FBI, however, "identified" a total of **five** hijackers, and claimed they were all assigned to seats in row **8.**

None of the names of the hijackers originally appeared on any of the publicly released passenger manifests.

Curious......

[Sources: http://www.whatreallyhappened.com;
http://latimes.com/news.nationworld/
nation/la100601probe.story;
http://www.madison.com/attack/loganair.php;
http://www.whatreallyhappened.com/lindex2.html]

Advice to Bush & Bin Laden

A pupil asked Kungfutse's son, "Anything he tells you he ain't told us?"

Son thought, said: Told me to study poetry. Said, without poetry can't find words for inarticulate heart wisdom. Another time he told me to study music. Said, without music outside, never find harmony inside.

Pupil said: Lucky bloke I am, ask one question and learn three things. Learn to study poetry, learn to study music, and learn the wise man does not nag his son.

— from the *Lun Yu*

THE PERILS OF COCAINE ABUSE

Two recent political leaders allegedly had this nefarious habit.

Both came to power after dubious elections, by non-electoral and irregular methods.

Both nations immediately experienced attacks on famous public buildings.

Both leaders blamed an ethnic minority before forensics had any evidence.

Both led "witch-hunts" against the accused minority.

Both suspended civil liberties "temporarily."

Both put the citizenry under surveillance.

Both maintained secret and clandestine governments.

Both launched wars against most of the world.

One had a funny mustache. Can you name the other one?

**the
Farben
works
still
intact**

FIENDISH PLOTS

Fu who?   — *The Fiendish Plot of Dr. Fu Manchu*

Last night I looked at *The Fiendish Plot of Dr. Fu Manchu* on TV, partly because it starred Peter Sellers as both Dr. Fu and his enemy Nayland Smith of Scotland Yard, and partly because I wanted to compare the epic battle between Fu and Smith with the current rumble between Dubya and Osama bin Laden.

I have long regarded Dr. Fu as both archetype and stereotype— the incarnation of British fear of Oriental revenge for imperialist invasions. Osama fits that role very well indeed, and the Dubya/ Smith parallel came across with almost synchronistic shock:

"The difference between Fu and me," Smith sez, "is that I'm Good and he's Evil."

Have Dubya's speech-writers read the original Fu Manchu novels or just seen this film?

Unlike the novels, the film does not portray Dr. Fu as driven by "motiveless malignancy" (like Dubya explaining Osama: "He is a man who is an evil man.") On the contrary, Fu has a personal grudge we can understand: as a boy he had to work in his father's laundry at Eton, and starching all those white collars drove him bonkers. That makes more sense to me as a novelist than the unmotivated malice of Osama, as portrayed by Dubya, CNN and the other corporate spin doctors.

Fear not, O true believers: the film didn't mention imperialism, any more than the novels—or Dubya's speech-writers.

Meanwhile, another of my favorite villains has resurfaced:

The Fiendish Plot of Ming the Merciless

[Adapted from the Irish Times 5 November 2001]

The cannabis campaigner, "Ming the Merciless", has been arrested in Dublin this afternoon in connection with posting what is believed to be cannabis to close to 300 politicians and journalists.

He was detained while attempting to hand deliver a potted cannabis plant to the offices of a senior Government Minister, and taken to Pearse Street Garda station where he is being held under Section 4 of the Criminal Justice Act.

Earlier today, several letters containing what is believed to be cannabis and addressed to politicians at their offices were discovered by officials checking the post following recent anthrax scares.

"Ming the Merciless", whose real name is Luke Flanagan from County Roscommon, is a well-known campaigner for the legalisation of cannabis. He ran in Galway West on a legalise cannabis ticket during the 1997 general election and also ran on the same platform in the European Parliamentary elections in the constituency of Connacht-Ulster.

Every country gets the villains it deserves. And as Joyce would say, there's lots of fun in Flanagan's work.

PEARL HARBOR REDUX?

Of the five passengers the FBI originally identified as the highjackers of American Airlines Flight 11, no fewer than three have turned up alive in the Mideast. The TSOG has even admitted this error, and said the terrorists used fake ID. The FBI immediately substituted seven new (Middle Eastern-named) suspects. What evidence could they possibly have had, to immediately implicate seven new suspects? It gives one ferociously to wonder...

[Sources: http://worldmessenger.20m.com/alive.html
http://www.mujahideen.fsnet.co.uk/wtc/wtc-hijackers.htm
http://news.bbc.co.uk/hi/english/world/middle_east/
newsid_1559000/1559151.stm]

The NYC Police Dept. claims to have found a passport from one of the hijackers, eight blocks away from World Trade Center. Faith-based citizens must now try to believe the passport somehow managed to miraculously survive the raging infernos of the WTC towers, and float to the ground, unscathed.

This convenient miracle was repeated in Pennsylvania, where a terrorist suicide note was "discovered" by FBI investigators, near the smoldering crater of the crash site, despite Flight 93 (in the words of the FBI) being "vaporized" on impact.

[Sources: http://www.cnn.com/2001/US/09/16/
gen.america.under.attack/
http://www.commondreams.org/view01/0929-07.htm]

Morals in the Market Place

An October issue of *Moscow Times* profiled Ms. Galine Sinit-syna, 40, who is unemployed (formerly, a firing-range instructor), supports a teen-age son, and feels her job prospects are dim. She is a few months too old for the military but would really like to become a government sniper in Chechnya, which she has heard pays about $60 a day plus a per-kill commission.

She said she has tried to take the high moral ground in her job search, turning down a very lucrative position as a contract killer for the mob.

[*Moscow Times,* October 2, 2001]

Profits Con

In December, the Days Inn hotel in Hicksville, NY (near JFK airport), agreed to a fine and refunds to settle charges that, in the days after Sept. 11, it billed people stranded by the air-travel shut-down up to $399 a day for its $139 rooms. And The *New York Times* reported in October that Providence Inc., a Cincinnati firm that lends money to victims in anticipation of litigation, sent at least 76 relatives of September 11 victims portfolios containing gifts of up to $200, along with a list of suggested lawyers. And New York City police arrested 115 unlicensed Ground Zero vendors in December and cracked down on many more vendors for selling counterfeit logo items of the NYPD and Fire Department of New York (counterfeiting that denied proceeds to the police and firefighter foundations that control the trademarks).

[Sources: CNN.com, 12-27-01; New York Times, 10-13-01; New York Times, 12-14-01; New York Post, 1-9-02; all via *News of the Weird*]

Funny Coincidences

Some evidence links the Venice, Florida-based Huffman Aviation flight school (responsible for training the hijackers on AA

Flight 11) to the C.I.A., as well as certain "Christian charities." In fact, the very same Middle Eastern hijackers that allegedly took control of AA Flight 11, attended classes at flight schools in both Venice and Sarasota, Florida, and were trained by the very same instructors who have routinely flown world-wide missions for various Christian fundamentalist missionary services including Pat Robertson's "Operation Blessing" and Jerry Falwell's "World Help," both ardent supporters of Bushware 2.0...

[Sources: http://www.onlinejournal.com/Special_Reports/
Hopsicker030202/hopsicker030202.htm;
http://onlinejournal.com/Special_Reports/Hopsicker100201/
hopsi http://www.madcowprod.com/]

WHY HANNIBAL LECTER WOULD MAKE A BETTER PRESIDENT THAN GEORGE W. BUSH

Koan

How do you handle your rage?
— Dr. Lecter's last question to Clarice in
The Silence of the Lambs (the book, not the movie)

Parable

The other night I dreamed of myself riding a crowded New York subway, standing and holding a handgrip. I got off at Avenue of the Americas and entered an office building. Suddenly I found myself not walking but in my current wheel-chair—a dream leap of 40 years—but still, as in my 20s, working at a job that profoundly bored me.

A cheerful and friendly receptionist wheeled me to an executive with whom I had an appointment. Then I suddenly had a total memory lapse and could not remember why I had to see this man or even what I should say. With deep humiliation I realized that I had gotten lost in daydreams about the books I wanted to write and lost track of my "real" job. I felt, as I often did in my 20s, incompetent, "maladjusted," a born failure, *Americanus nondesirabilis*.

Suddenly the executive turned into Hannibal Lecter and we sat drinking coffee and discussing literature in a Paris cafe. He wore the snappy Panama hat with an exquisite Armani suit that he had sported in *Hannibal*—the movie, not the book. I told him that the writers I enjoy most (Swift, Twain, Bierce, Faulkner, Joyce, Pound, Chandler, Higgins) all contained a special flavor of satire that I could not precisely define even though I think it permeates my own books; "acid satire" hardly seemed satisfactory.

"I think I have the word you need," Dr. Lecter said genially. "Biting. You write biting satire." And he showed his small white teeth in a gentle smile.

Thesis

Everybody knows that the President of the United States at this time in history needs to have the personality and temperament of a serial killer. Of course, many people do not like to hear the matter stated so bluntly, and prefer euphemisms, but we all know that a modern president has to kill lots and lots of people, right? We all agree on that. And he can't hesitate or dilly-dally about it (Carter's Folly); that shows "squeaky softness."

(My use of "he" and "man" does not signify "unconscious sexism." An America with a woman president would have changed so much that no current generalizations could predict it.)

According to the corporate media, which allows all shades of opinion from the far right to the middle-of-the road, America has vicious enemies on all continents (except maybe Antarctica). These Evildoers, driven by Satan, want to destroy us and take all we own.

Hence, by this analysis, our president must have no compunction about spilling blood; in short, like it or not, he must have the soul—or soullessness—of a serial killer.

A rival "leftish" view, banned from the corporate media but widely available on Internet, holds that the world does not consist entirely of endless enemies, but does contain many, many peoples who want to get out from under the heel of the IMF, the World Bank and the multi-nationals. "Our" government, in this view, actually belongs not to us but to these giant money-cows, who finance the two major parties and ensure that no third party ever gets decent coverage in their media. The government then acts as Company Cop for the rich, suppressing all attempts at rebellion or national liberation, etc. Thus, once again, *via* a dissenting ideology, we arrive at the conclusion that the president must think, feel and act like a serial killer.

The only pragmatic (non-theoretical) issue that can divide us then remains only: what kind or flavor of serial killer do we want in the oval office? Or, even more pragmatically, what sort of serial killer can best represent the rich who pay campaign expenses?

I think Hannibal Lecter, M.D. would satisfy me, and might even satisfy the owners and proprietors of USCorp, much better than George W. Bush. Do we want a bumbling amateur or a man who really has a talent as well as a relish for multiple homicide?

I can see no room for debate here. The Lyin' Scion may have killed a hell of a lot more people than Hannibal, by a margin of about 2000 to one, but he does it without flair or zest. Hannibal really puts his heart and soul into the work, and even adds a touch of surrealist humor at times.

Consider also the other functions of the president.

In the first place, since we like to pretend that we still have a democracy here, I assert that Dr. Lecter could win an election honestly, without any of the taint of felony that blemishes Shrub, who lost the popular vote and won by malodorous and questionable electoral votes in Florida. Dr. Lecter, by contrast, seems an honest box office smash, his latest film grossing $100,000,000 in its first week alone. He obviously has more fans than His Royal Fraudulency George II.

Note also that Dr. Lecter speaks correct and even eloquent English (despite his Lithuanian birth) whereas Boy George babbles like an idiot. Who will command more respect from the educated peoples of the world?

Hannibal has several languages—French, Italian, Spanish, Lithuanian etc.—whereas King George the Turd can barely speak English. Who could make livelier conversation with the leaders, ambassadors etc. of foreign nations? Who would make a better impression?

Again: at age 64 (born 1938), Hannibal looks and acts like the archetype of the Elder Statesman. W reminds most of us of Giggles the Clown.

It seems highly doubtful that Dead Brain Talking could discuss anything more complex than *Fun With Dick and Jane*. Dr. Lecter can often recite the exact chemical formula for the neuro-psychological ailments of his patients; he can, and does, give a scholarly lecture—in correct Tuscan—on the moral theology of Dante; he works part-time on a mathematical critique of Hawkins' attempted unification of quantum mechanics and general relativity; he has wide artistic interests and plays the harpsichord with a real feel for the music; etc. Since the wider the mental landscape, the more balanced the judgment, we could expect him to act more prudently than Bushware 2.0.

Hannibal Lecter has *already* become a more civilizing influence on this barbaric nation than Our Anencephalic Emperor. See for example http://mischanet.net/llf_main.html where Lecterphiles have begun to assemble online all the art and music Hannibal especially cherishes. The epiphany of hordes of horror buffs suddenly and ardently turning on to high art and high culture might even indicate what Jung would call "a shift in the constella-tion of the archetypes." All our Resident Putz might offer along those lines would make a donkey weep and an owl laugh out loud.

Dr. Lecter also has a wonderful, if somewhat fey, sense of whimsy—a possible virtue in a world as mad as this. Witness his Jesus Christ wrist-watch—just like a Mickey Mouse watch but even more in tune with compassionate conservatism. By contrast, President Beelzebush has as much wit as a box of kitty-litter.

Of course, I must admit that Dr. Lecter occasionally acts rashly. He has already eaten the frontal lobes of a candidate for Congress and might devour a few Senators if they seriously piss him off. Well, who needs frontal lobes in Congress, anyway? And we would certainly have a more rational government absent a few of the archeological specimens in the Senate...

Of course, this whole issue of cannibalism remains problemat-ical, and might seriously disturb those dubbed "effete intellectuals" by Spiro Agnew. Personally, I favor a cannibal president on both surrealist and realist grounds. As Rev. Jonathan Swift pointed out in his "A Modest Proposal" over 200 years ago, cannibalism should pose no moral issue for those who tolerate imperialism, for if "we" (or some of us) devour the natural resources of a nation, why not devour its people also? Why consider it more ethical to let them die of filth, squalor and starvation?

Swift's views appear echoed in both Pound's *Cantos* and Burroughs's *Naked Lunch.* Those who can't read should have a chance to grok fully what's on the end of that long TV fork before they swallow it. Accepting a cannibal president might qualify as the most educational experience in a hundred years or more.

Besides, Dr. Lecter always acts as a gourmet, not a gourmand; although Sir Anthony Hopkins has "put on some weight" as they say, the novels always describe Hannibal as "slim." At most, we might expect him to ingest a few Senators, as mentioned above, and maybe a couple of dozen head of bureaucrats. Well, perhaps a few TV evangelists, too. None of this would amount to a great loss, and the educational benefits in making American politics totally explicit still seem enormous to me. As it says in *Mong-Tse*, "Is there any difference between killing a man with a sword and killing him with a club? Is there any difference between killing him with a sword and killing him with a system of economics?"

Dr. Lecter as president would help make this ancient Oriental wisdom comprehensible to all.

However, one question remains. Dr. Lecter despises those who kill for money (he despises avarice in general); would he blindly take orders and kill those the owners of America want killed? Just for a paycheck? I think this poses no real problem. They just have to let Hannibal pick the times for the bombings or invasions. His ironic humor would prevail and he would launch his wars at the hour the natives attend church. This would give him a load of new clippings for his famous scrapbook of horrible and gruesome things that happened to people at prayer.

COPULATING CURRENCY

Neurosemantics and Money

> People sometimes ask me, "Do you have to use that kind
> of language, Dr. Bandler?" And I tell them "Fuck, yes!"
> — Richard Bandler, Ph.D.

James Joyce defined an artistic epiphany as any "vulgarity of
language" which reveals the "whatness" or "radiance" of an event
or of those structural systems which remain "grave and constant in
human affairs." As biographer Richard Ellmann noted, the effect of
these fragments of conversation, preserved in Joyce's novels, often
appears "uncanny." I myself tend to find them a combination of the
tragic and the hilarious.

Last December I experienced a Joycean epiphany—combining
the uncanny, the tragic and the hilarious—while looking at TV—
and wrote it up as a "Thought for the Month" on my website
(http//www.rawilson.com), as follows:

I WANT MY FUCKING MONEY
**"Shit, motherfucker! I want my fucking money,
motherfucker!"**

Last night I looked at Spike Lee's superb film *Jungle Fever* on
the Independent Film Channel and that line hurtled off the TV and
burned into my neurons like a Joycean epiphany. The speaker, a
minor character in the story, virtually a non-character, spoke into a
cell-phone as the major character walked past him in a crowd
scene, and yet he seemingly summed up everything about our
world today.

171

Joyce developed his theory of the artistic epiphany from a similarly simple sentence that he overheard passing an open window in Dublin circa 1900. It seemed to him that with his usual mixture of logic, empathy and artistic intuition he "knew in a flash" a great many things about the speakers, their lives, the lives of most Dubliners and, by extension, the lives of colonized peoples everywhere. I invite you to apply the same methods to the wonderful sentence Mr. Lee has given us:

> Shit, motherfucker! I want my fucking money, motherfucker!

In the feudal age, people once fought wars over Land, when Land served as the source of wealth. Those who had Land wanted more, on the usual addictive rule that we want more of what makes us feel very, very good. They also worried that others wanted to take their Land away. Then paper Money appeared, almost as abstract as pure information in communication theory. For over 400 years now, the world has struggled over Money—working for it, swindling and robbing for it, conspiring to monopolize it, going to war over it. Since less than one percent of Earthians owns 99 percent of the Money, the (approximately) six billion of the rest of us struggle evermore desperately over the one percent of the green magick not yet monopolized. We all feel like Spike Lee's guy on the cell-phone part of the time, do we not?

By the way 23 Zeus (23 December 2001 e.v.) marks the 36th birthday of former Special Agent Clarice Starling. *Bon appetit* to her and Hannibal both!

❧❦❧

I left this "open," hoping readers would decipher the full epiphany from my hints about coinage and cannibalism. After all, Joyce Himself simply recorded his epiphanies and did not perform exegesis upon them. I share his confidence in the intelligence of my readers.

Evidently, not all my readers deserve that confidence. Shortly after the above appeared I received a shocking response from The Prophets Conference, which had previously booked me for two lectures this year. They wrote:

> As you will not be joining the Monterey and Santa Fe conferences as faculty please remove these events from your website.
> I WANT MY FUCKING MONEY "Shit, motherfucker! I want my fucking money, motherfucker!"
> The opening lines of your web page are an example of why we have discontinued presenting your work. Even though you are quoting Spike Lee and leading to a significant point, we were set back by the above intro.
> This has increasingly become the case at the conferences. What we feel to be your important insights are being lost to the audience when packaged in hard and harsh language. It has become increasingly clear that this is not your audience. The complaints have become too numerous. They are not hearing you.
>
> Best regards,
>
> Robin

I haven't laughed so much since the hawgs et Mason Vergier; in fact, I almost fell out of my wheelchair. The Prophets' logophobia (fear of words) seemed to me a notable example of paleolithic neurosemantics, and I decided to share this second epiphany with a few friends. As a result, science-fiction author David Jay Brown (*Brainchild,* 1988 and *Virus: The Alien Strain,* 1999, both New Falcon Publications) wrote to the Prophets as follows:

> Dear Prophets,
>
> I was truly surprised, and deeply disappointed, to hear that you have removed Robert Anton Wilson from your list of speakers. I believe that he is one of the smartest and funniest people around. I have been deeply inspired

by Dr. Wilson's lectures and books, and consider him to be one of the most important philosophers that our species has yet produced.

Please remove me from your mailing list.

Thank You,

David Jay Brown

To which the Prophets replied, in full:

From: prophets <prophets@greatmystery.org>
To: David Jay Brown
Subject: Re: Robert Anton Wilson
Date: Thursday, February 14, 2002 9:12 AM

Go fuck yourself.

I wonder if this indicates that the Prophets do not superstitiously fear my words at all but rather dread the ideas I expound, especially after 911? I don't know...but let us examine Mr. Lee's epiphany more closely to see what fearful and loathsome menace this combination of words contains.

———

Remarks which appear crude or offensive in the instant may become, with a change of perspective, somewhere between droll and riotously funny.
                                    — Hannibal Lecter, M.D.

———

First of all, I note that every individual word comes from an Anglo-Saxon, Danish or Frissian root. Since the Norman conquests—of England in 1066 e.v. and Ireland 1169 e.v.—"liquid" words of French/Latin origin have dominated royal, aristocratic and legal circles, and the "harsher" Teutonic sounds remained predominant only among farmers, serfs and the generally *déclassé*. For instance, the rich still eat "mutton" (from the French) where the poor eat "lamb" (from the Saxon)—but both words denote the same non-verbal meat. Similarly, Clinton had "oral sex" in the Oval Office, but ordinary bums only have blow-jobs.

Thus, from the perspective of sociological linguist Giambatista Vico—Joyce's acknowledged teacher in these matters—the history of language contains a buried history of class war and ethnic conflict.

Translate Lee's dialogue into upper class (Latinized) speech—

Excrement, incestuous person. I require my copulating currency, incestuous person.

—and you produce a version ludicrously inappropriate to the lower-class setting of *Jungle Fever* but much less "offensive" to the old ladies (of both sexes) at ProphetsCon.

Looking even closer—and recalling Emerson's neo-Viconian discovery that every word contains a "fossilized poem":

"**Shit**," the first word of the speech, immediately signals territorial conflict, and thus probably dates from what Vico called the age of "half-bestial" humans (who survived, he believed, as the Bigfoot critters of North America). All mammals mark their territories with excretions, and our closest relatives among the primates often hurl feces at each other during border disputes. Later, the Conquerors—or Great Pirates (as Bucky Fuller called them)—learned to mark their turf with ink excretions on paper and hurl bombs instead of turds, but the vocabulary of the common soldiers remains relentlessly anal. "Ass," as Norman Mailer has documented, signifies the total personality ("I wanna get my ass out of here" does not mean that the speaker intends to leave the rest of his body behind) and "shit" means the total military environment ("all this shit.")

For more and a deeper analysis of this, see "The Anal Territorial Circuit" in my *Prometheus Rising* (New Falcon Publications, Tempe AZ).

"**...motherfucker**" represents the deadliest insult in Patriarchal society (Vico's sarcastically named "Heroic" epoch), and thus magnifies the warlike implications of "Shit." Since such insults/ threats survive chiefly among the conquered/enslaved, one already knows a great deal about the speaker even without looking at the TV screen.

"**I want my fucking money**" represents the informational—as distinct from emotional-territorial—part of the message, and carries us from the area of fossilized poetry to that of *accidental* poetry, in a way that Ezra Pound would have enjoyed as much as Joyce. "Fucking," of course, does not literally mean copulating here; it serves rather as what lexicographers call a general intensifier. But if we take it literally, a very funny poem appears and we decisively enter the modern age, where paper tickets have replaced Land as the arena of bloodiest struggle.

"Fucking money"—or copulating currency, as the Prophets would prefer—accidentally and poetically revives an issue that agitated philosophers and theologians from Aristotle to the late Renaissance: how can money, an inanimate object, reproduce itself? Only animals can reproduce, right? (Cf. "Or is your gold and silver ewes and rams?": Shakespeare, *The Merchant of Venice*, I, iii.) Through most of our history, majority opinion among the learned—the only opinion in all those centuries, I think; but I can't swear to that, not having read everything—held that this "miraculous multiplication" resulted from a species of fraud or swindle.

⇒◆⇐

Many, especially St. Ambrose, analyzed the fraud closely and decided that it rests upon a monopoly over the coin or currency. Hence the Banks of Piety which, like Shakespeare's Antonio, lent without charging interest, thereby abolishing or diminishing usury.

By 1692, the Banks of Piety had ceased to exist and people read Shakespeare only for his poetry, not his ideas. That year, William Paterson, founder of the Bank of England, boldly declared the miracle of miraculous multiplication in an advertisement to prospective share-holders, promising they would have "benefit of interest on all the moneys which the bank creates out of nothing." Ever since, we have lived in what La tour de Pin called "the Age of Usury." Others, more politely, call it Finance Capitalism. All of us, born in debt, remain in debt all of our lives and the debt will pass on to our posterity, multiplying not only miraculously but faster than bunny rabbits. Economists call it *compound interest.*

Money not only has learned the art of fucking, but even that of reproduction. The people who demonstrate against the World Bank and the International Monetary Fund have not invented an original and radical idea but merely rediscovered the view of most of the Western classics. (Since the classics got chucked out of Academe, this rediscovery marks a major intellectual event.)

As for the somewhat oblique Hannibal Lecter joke with which I ended my original essay: I refer you again to Rev. Jonathan Swift's "A Modest Proposal." He demonstrates with cold logic that **anybody who can stomach capitalism should not gag at cannibalism.**

PEARL HARBOR REDUX?

Sitting, literally, right next to some of the "hijack suspects," of AA Flight 11 was Daniel C. Lewin, an American citizen with dual Israeli citizenship, who was a former elite Israeli commando officer in a secret unit of the Israeli Defense Force called "Sayeret Mat'Kal."

While a member of the IDF, Mr. Lewin apparently had received extensive "anti-terrorism" training. Sayeret Mat'Kal was formed in 1957, and explicitly created to infiltrate enemy territories; members of this unit are trained on the finer points of "looking and thinking like an Arab," and have been charged with conducting numerous death-squad killings, disguised as civilians.

Curiouser and curiouser......

[Sources: http://www.worldnetdaily.com/news/
article.asp?ARTICLE_ID=26676;
http://www.israelinsider.com/channels/
politics/articles/pol_0051.htm;
http://www.worldnetdaily.com/news/
article.asp?ARTICLE_ID=26626;
http://www.specwarnet.com/world/matkal.htm;
http://www.hoovers.com/co/capsule/6/0,2163,59556,00.html]

THOUGHTS TO PONDER

If you can't say the word "Fuck," you can't say "Fuck the Prophet's Conference."

— Ted Kane

I don't know what the fuck "improper language" means.

— Bob Geldorf

If you can't say FUCK in public, then the terrorists have won.

— D. Scott Apel

They Seek Him Here, They Seek Him There—

He is—you know, as I mention in my speeches—I do mention the fact that this is a fellow who is willing to commit youngsters to their death. And he, himself, tries to hide, if, in fact, he's hiding at all. So I don't know where he is.

— G.W. Bush, in response to a question about why the President rarely mentions Osama Bin Laden in speeches, Washington, DC, March 13, 2002; CNN transcript.

It's because they're stupid. That's why everyone does everything.

— Homer Simpson

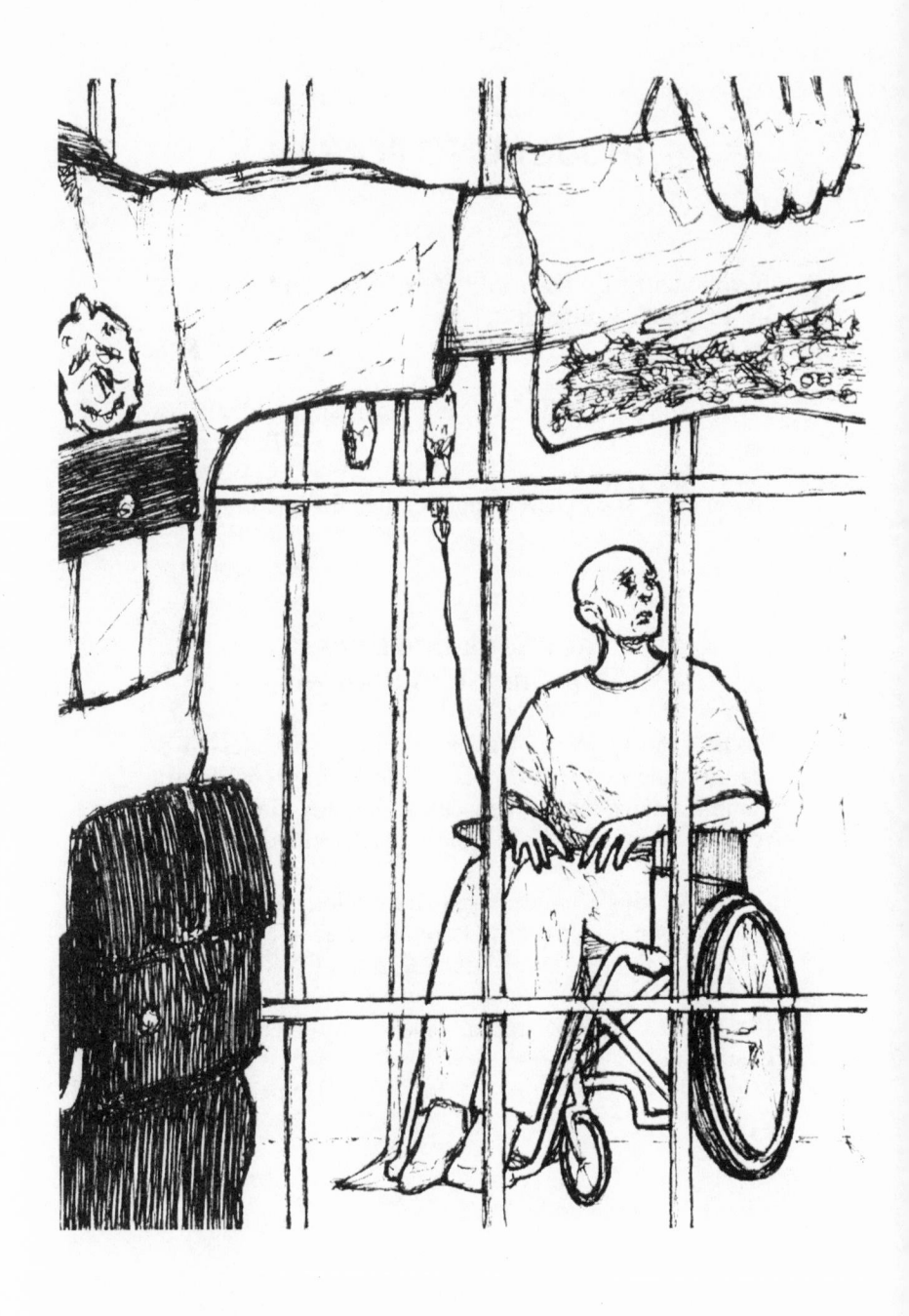

CANCER PATIENT ASKS, "SHOULD I BE ARRESTED?"
Hutchinson Doesn't Answer

ROCKVILLE, MARYLAND—Medical marijuana patients, frustrated by the U.S. Drug Enforcement Administration's contradictory and sometimes inaccurate statements regarding medical marijuana, confronted DEA Administrator Asa Hutchinson during an appearance in Rockville, Maryland, this evening. Hutchinson left the event early in an apparent attempt to avoid further questioning.

Hutchinson appeared at the Barnes and Noble bookstore in Rockville's Montrose Crossing shopping center, in what was advertised as a "community discussion" with Cindy Mogil, author of "Swallowing a Bitter Pill: How Prescription and Over-the-Counter Drug Abuse is Ruining Lives—My Story".

Lawrence Silberman, who found that marijuana was the only medicine that allowed him to endure the harsh side effects of high-dose chemotherapy for non-Hodgkins lymphoma—a lethal and difficult-to-treat form of cancer—asked Hutchinson directly, "Do you think people like myself should be arrested, sir?"

Hutchinson responded vaguely, saying "the DEA is not in the habit of going after individual users." He repeatedly failed to answer directly, despite follow-ups from Bruce Mirken, director of communications of the Marijuana Policy Project, and Fernando Mosquera, a freshman at the University of Maryland, College Park. Mosquera described how marijuana helped him cope with the debilitating symptoms of Crohn's disease in a poignant column in the March 11 *Baltimore Sun*.

Hutchinson repeated claims that "science has not yet come to consensus" on the advantages of marijuana—similar to claims he made in justifying February DEA raids on medical marijuana providers in California. He did not acknowledge the Institute of Medicine's 1999 report, commissioned by the White House drug Tsar's office, which stated, "Nausea, appetite loss, pain and anxiety...all can be mitigated by marijuana." The report pointed out that "there is no clear alternative for people suffering from chronic conditions that might be relieved by smoking marijuana"—and urged that marijuana be made legally available to such patients on a case-by-case basis.

Hutchinson then took advantage of the first pause in the proceedings to leave early, ducking out without good-byes or acknowledgments of any kind.

March 18, 2002 e.v.

[Source: Marijuana Policy Project <mpp@mpp.org>]

BENEFITS OF FAITH-BASED ORGANIZATIONS

Men never do evil so completely and cheerfully as when they do it from religious conviction.
— Blaise Pascal (1623–1662)

How good bad music and bad reasons sound when one marches against an enemy!
— Friedrich Nietzsche, *Dawn* (1881)

Dressed to Kill

Saudi Arabia's religious police are reported to have forced schoolgirls back into a blazing building because they were not wearing Islamic head scarves and black robes.

Saudi newspapers said scuffles broke out between firemen and members of the Commission for the Promotion of Virtue and Prevention of Vice who tried to keep the girls inside a burning school in Mecca. Fifteen girls were killed as they stampeded to escape from the blazing building in the Muslim holy city.

Well, at least they left modest cadavers...

[Source: Daily Telegraph (London), 15 March 2002]

MASK & ANTI-MASK

UNDISCLOSED LOCATION—Decrying various unspecified aspects of the U.S. Shadow Government, an indeterminate number of Shadow Protesters gathered outside the organization's mountain retreat, sealed germ-free vault, or underground bunker, on Monday. "We unfortunately cannot comment on our feelings about the Shadow Government at this time," said an unnamed protester, neither confirming nor denying reports that he or she accused the Shadow Government of violating the U.S. Constitution.

After 20 minutes of protest, the group was dispersed by members of the Shadow Secret Service, who used "means at their disposal."

[Source: http://www.theonion.com/]

Enduring Freedom

Connecticut state Rep. Kevin Ryan, freshly sentenced to four months' hard time as a recidivist DUI, said he can very well conduct his legislative business from his cell and does not intend to resign.

[Source: *Buffalo News*, 17 September 2001]

MORE BENEFITS OF FAITH-BASED ORGANIZATIONS

"What amateurs we all are compared to Him..."

KABUL—U.S. jets struck the Afghan capital Friday on the Muslim day of prayer, rocking the city with huge explosions and reportedly blasting a Red Cross compound for a second time this month.

Three children were killed in overnight attacks on the city, hospital officials said.

After another night of sometimes intense bombing, three huge detonations shook Kabul at midday, raising clouds of smoke from the direction of the airport and the Khair Khana district to the north. It was unclear where the third explosion occurred.

One of the blasts struck a compound of the International Committee of the Red Cross, according to security guard Abdul Shakour.

He said warehouses used to store humanitarian supplies were damaged and stocks of rice, beans, blankets and oil were on fire. The compound was hit during an attack Oct. 16.

During late night bombing Thursday, three children were killed—two from one family living in the northwest area of the city and a third from the east part of town, officials at the Wazir Akbar Khan Hospital said.

During a sermon at a Kabul mosque Friday, an Islamic cleric said the "infidel hit our nation, even on Friday. They are very unkind to our people."

"In the name of Allah, the All-merciful, the Everlas—
AWWWRRRRK!!"

Two days after USCorp terrorists killed Moslems at worship in a mosque in Afghanistan, Moslem terrorists killed Roman Catholics at worship in a cathedral in Pakistan.

"In the Name of the Father and of the Son and of the Ho—

ARRRRGH!"

[Source: http://www.stopnato.org.uk AP. 26 October 2001]

YET MORE BENEFITS OF FAITH-BASED ORGANIZATIONS

Faith & Journalism

BELFAST (AP)—A shadowy Protestant gang claimed responsibility Saturday for shooting to death a Catholic investigative journalist, the first such slaying in the 30-year history of Northern Ireland's conflict.

The killing of Martin O'Hagan, 51, as he walked home from a pub in his home town of Lurgan raised pressure on Britain to crack down on outlawed Protestant groups, which are supposed to be observing ceasefires in support of Northern Ireland's struggling 1998 peace accord.

Blasphemy

LONDON, UK, 21 August 2001 (AI)—Following the court ruling in the case of Dr. Younus Sheikh, Amnesty International said it is appalled that yet another innocent person has been convicted of blasphemy and sentenced to death.

"The charges were maliciously brought, the allegations did not establish blasphemy and the trial which led to the conviction on such grounds could not have been fair," the organization said.

"The blasphemy laws of Pakistan are a handy tool to silence debate and dissent. They are also used to detain people when the real motivation includes land issues or professional rivalry. In the interest of justice, the blasphemy laws should be abolished or, as a first step, amended to prevent abuse."

Only last month, a Christian man, Ayub Masih, had his death sentence for blasphemy confirmed by the High Court. Amnesty

International believes that the real motive for bringing the blasphemy charge was a land dispute in his village.

[Source: http://www.InformationTimes.com]

AN INTERVIEW WITH A BULGARIAN MAGAZINE

INA: Hellllo, dear Bob.

BOB: Hellllllllllo dear Ina.

INA: As you probably (don't) remember from my first mail, I am an editor at the leading lifestyle magazine in Bulgaria (sor-ry). *Prometheus Rising* just came out here and I've already seen the translation of *Sex, Drugs, and Magick* and my Thinker thinks you are God, and now my Prover is working on proving it.

BOB: Not a god. Not even a mullah. Just an ordinary elderly widower with a gaudy vocabulary.

INA: I worship you and if we were face to face, I would have done the muslim bowing with extended arms for you.

BOB: That would seriously embarrass me...

INA: You have helped me understand so many things about my life and visions and feelings and all, that it will take a whole book to describe.

BOB: Thank you. Some regard me as a philosopher, some as a public nuisance. That question remains open. I think Nietzsche believed "philosopher" and "public nuisance" constitute two names for the same occupation. But I consider myself basically an artist/humorist who occasionally writes essays, which some regard as philosophy and some as the ravings of a disordered mind. I've written a lot of fiction, epics even, and some poetry I don't totally repent and even a few plays, none of them translated to Bulgarian...yet.

INA: So, I am pretty stunned and I will have trouble doing a good interview over the mail, but maybe if you send me some answers and then I fill in another set of questions that I would have asked, were I to hear the answers directly—and you answer the second set—and I ask a third... Kidding...

BOB: Allah be praised, the All-merciful.

INA: But really, could you kindly try and make it sound like it was taken live, and not give me one- or two-word answers. Rather, picture me sitting in front of you—beautiful, blond, blue eyed and gullible as I am—and add in some why's and how's and when's and where's for me, whenever possible. And make the answers longer than normal written speech, and sprinkle it with your outburst of terrific humor—I hope it's OK with you.

BOB: Well, I can't turn humor off and on like a faucet in a sink, but I'll try not to become too boring.

INA: Thanks, I'm already building a shrine to you over here.

BOB: Make it abstract. All idols have Klee feet.

INA: And, if you could do it very fast, like in two days, it would be great because I am closing the next issue then, and I really wanted it to come out this time, while the book is still red-hot and everything. So here are the questions: What was the first experience that made you doubt your own reality tunnel is everybody's reality?

BOB: I guess it happened around age 10—circa 1942. My mother bought new curtains and insisted they "were" green, but they looked blue to me. Then I began to notice at baseball games that the fans of one team never "saw" the same space-time events as the fans of the other team. At around the age of 18 (c. 1950) I read Alfred Korzybski's *Science and Sanity*, which explained why no two observers ever perceive the same "reality." You might say that the psychedelic revolution of the 1960's only confirmed what I already suspected.

INA: Your first LSD trip—when, where, who with? Was it fun or too scary? Basic outline of the insights it gave you.

BOB: On my first psychedelic trip, I used peyote, not acid. I'd call the experience ecstatic, erotic, mystical, thoroughly delightful and very, very, very, very, very educational.

Major insights? [1] We never got ejected from the Garden of Eden; it's all around us, right here, right now. We're just too full of words and opinions to notice it. [2] Relativity extends far beyond Einstein's physics. Neurological relativism explains more than instrumental relativism. The nervous system, in fact, acts as the instrument that reads (and interprets) all other instruments. As Lily Tomlin says, "We're all in this alone."

INA: Do you support the Hundredth Monkey Theory (when the monkeys that have learned to wash a potato reach a certain percentage of all members of the species, even if they inhabit an isolated island and have no contact with the rest, ALL monkeys of the species learn to wash potatoes) and how does it apply to your theories?

BOB: I believe the Hundredth Monkey case never happened; it's sort of folklore.[9] Other cases, in the works of biologist Rupert Sheldrake, seem much better documented. These cases, and my own psychedelic research, incline me to suspect that some sort of energy-system of nonlocal character exists everywhere in and beyond space-time and contains all the local systems each of us calls "me" or "my mind." I consider *energy* as primary; and *information,* the ordering of energy into signals, as the foundation of language, math, science etc.—everything we "inherit" as members of a verbalizing species. In other words, the ordering of energy into signals produces sociological evolution. Those who control signals control humanity. That explains why every government tries to block signals it finds uncongenial, and why Internet has driven them all batty. The very possibility of group ESP might drive them ballistic.

INA: What sense (vision, taste, smell) would you have enhanced forever, if it were possible?

BOB: Why stop at one? I've expanded all of them a wee bit and I'd like to expand them to infinity. Dogs smell more of the world than we do, but I don't want to become a dog forever; I

---

[9] Bob is too kind. The "phenomenon" was first "described" by Lyall Watson in his book, *Lifetide* (1979). It was further "reported" by Ken Keyes, Jr. in *The Hundredth Monkey* (1982) to support the notion that we can prevent nuclear war if enough of us think good thoughts. After the Watson/Keyes story had been totally debunked, Watson said that he had made the story up. ("It is a metaphor of my own making, based on very slim evidence and a great deal of hearsay. I have never pretended otherwise.") Nonetheless, the "phenomenon" is (still!!) quoted as *scientific fact.* (See, for example, Tim Ray's discussion of the causes and cures of the 9-11 attacks at http://www.beamteam. com/peace2.htm.) [Ed.]

prefer to reverse that and occasionally become a god. On the other hand, unlike dog/god, BOB remains the same forward and backward, so I can enjoy my total BOBness just as I am.

INA: Did you ever have trouble with the authorities?

BOB: Well, I've gotten tear-gassed several times during anti-war protests, and arrested once for anti-segregation activity, but by and large I don't think the "'authorities" consider me important. That's okay; I don't consider them important either. Science and art seem important to me; politics seems like a visit to the monkey house at the zoo. Except for the apes having some nasty new weapons, it makes a great comedy, especially for fans of the Three Stooges and *Finnegans Wake.*

INA: Have you ever had a bad trip? What happened?

BOB: I tried belladonna, because a friend told me "it's just like peyote." In my experience, nothing like peyote happened. Blue and green curtains again, you know? It may have seemed like peyote to him, but it seemed like bloody hell to me. I would describe that awful night as 14 hours of paranoid schizophrenia. Demons and Nazis and monsters of all sorts. Even my wife grew fangs and turned into a vampire... I never tried belladonna again and never will; and I'd never recommend it to anyone—except George W. Bush and Osama bin Laden. They deserve it.

INA: Your latest "all-things-are-the-same-size" kind of revelation that could also be considered total idiocy, depending on the reader?

BOB: I have lately begun to perceive/conceive history as Selfish Gene Pools at war. Gene pools do not have the intelligence of their individual members. Gene pools act on a level between a 4-year-old problem child and a mammalian herd. (Dawkins made his theory of the Selfish Gene work, or seem to, by shifting the meaning of "selfish" at strategic moments but I don't think I have done that.) When I say "selfish" I mean what everybody else means. Gene pools kill each other—genocide. Gene pools plot mischief against each other continually. Gene pools have no ethics whatsoever; they have "patriotism." The first step to conscious humanity consists of developing some kind of moral vision unlinked to any gene pool or pools you accidentally got born into.

Now, do you want to consider that a serious contribution to sociobiology, a parody of same, or just my latest Cosmic Schmuckery?

INA: Did you expect to start such a revolution?

BOB: Strangely enough, I did. I suspect that all artists have the vanity to want to change the world, but most of us eventually develop enough common sense not to announce such egomania in public. But I got stoned once in London with an interviewer and told her that Art can't save us now so I aim at Magick. Damn, it got into the *Times* next day.

The London Fucking *Times*.

I almost changed my name and hid in a cave after that.

Damn right, I want to change the world.

It badly needs update and upgrade.

INA: Tell me something intriguing about Timothy Leary—you knew him for how long? Something he did or said? What made him special, did he have any bad habits and funny sides?

BOB: I knew Dr. Leary for 30 years (1964–1994). When he had his final illness, the last words we exchanged went like this: "Tim, I've met Buckminster Fuller, and I still consider you the most intelligent human I know. I've met George Carlin, and I still consider you the funniest person alive. " And he looked up at me and gave that Irish grin and said, "Bob, you're an excellent judge of character." Two days later he died.

I think visiting Tim in prison in the 1970's, and visiting him when the cancer got him in the 1990's, taught me lessons about courage and humor that have helped me immeasurably in my own griefs and troubles.

Oh, yes, he could act like a sonofabitch at times, but only under extreme pressure.

INA: Who was the person you interviewed for *Playboy* that made you the greatest impression? How, why? Something funny from that period?

BOB: I never interviewed anybody for *Playboy*; I edited "The Playboy Forum," which preached mind-your-own-business libertarianism and get-the-government-off-our-fronts.

INA: How will recent events (11 September) affect the relative freedom that fans of tripping substances enjoy right now?

BOB: Tripping never became even *relatively* free in the United States, since the government banned it in 1966. Even scientific research in that area remains illegal. The Holy Inquisition did not end in 1819, as most historians claim; the U.S. government has taken over where the Vatican left off. In one of our States—Kansas—biology instructors can't even teach evolution. Imagine Afghanistan with Christian Fundamentalists in control instead of Muslim Fundamentalists and that gives you an idea of U.S.A. under Bushware 2.0.

INA: Do you have a theory about what happened and why?

BOB: I have several theories, none of which I believe. I don't suppose we'll learn "the truth"—or an approximation thereof—for at least 20 years.

Meanwhile, my favorite (tentative) model sees this in terms of Selfish Gene Pools. One gene pool—which I call the DEA, or the House of Orange—consists of intermarried *D*utch-*E*nglish-*A*merican "royal" families and bankers. They have increasingly owned and governed the planet over the past 400 years. In the opinion of the non-DEA majority, this clan has disgracefully mismanaged damned near EVERYTHING. Osama bin Laden represents an Arabic gene pool that has particularly bitter grudges against the DEA. I consider bin Laden a religious nut case; if he had any sense, he'd try to recruit the entire Third World (4 billion people) all of whom have their own grudges against the Orange Mob. Instead, he only appeals to the Muslims (one billion). He'll lose, but somebody else will learn from his error. The non-white, non-Christian majority will not stop struggling against the World Bank and other DEA control machines. That's why Bush keeps reminding us that this war has no foreseeable end.

INA: Is U.S.A. becoming a police state as a reaction? Are people getting paranoid?

BOB: I think the U.S.A. has already become a police state. It started with the National Security Act of 1947, became exquisitely perfected by the War Against Some Drugs, and they buried the Bill of Rights with a stake through its heart with the USA PATRIOT

Act. Just like Rome: Republic to Empire to "the Barbarians are at the gates."

INA: Could the world be heading towards a matriarchal society?

BOB: I doubt it. I think we'll become a worldround decentralized Internet community with "government" operating locally in groups of appropriate size for each task. Bloody anarchy. Each cell solving local problems and blocs of cells organized for bigger problems. Some blocs may become matriarchal, some may remain patriarchal, but most, I think, will become egalitarian. All run by "contract," mutual agreement. Meanwhile, I feel very happy that Internet can survive nuclear war even. It will become the brain of humanity.

INA: Does life get boring at a certain point?

BOB: I never find anything boring, even loneliness. Boredom results from insufficient attention.

INA: What's mankind's problem right now?

BOB: Too much midbrain activity (mammalian conditioning) and not enough forebrain activity (human creativity).

INA: How could you be the only person I know with a happy marriage?

BOB: I found the only woman who could tolerate living with me for 42 years.

INA: What do you know that the rest of us don't?

BOB: The real names of the Three Stooges: Moishe Horwitz, Jerome Horwitz and Laurence Feinstein.

INA: What is the greatest sin?

BOB: Believing in "sin." It always makes people torture themselves and often drives them to murder others.

INA: What is the magic word?

BOB: Fnord!

INA: What is the question you haven't found an answer to and you wish you had?

BOB: Which room did I leave my glasses in?

**the
Farben
works
still
intact**

FROM THE DEATH-CELLS@PISA...

Haec sunt fastae
    Under Taishan quatorze Juilet
with the hill ablaze north of Taishan
and Amber Rives is dead, the end of that chapter
      see Time for June 25th
Mr Graham himself unmistably,
      on a horse, an ear and a beard's point showing
and the Farben works still intact
    — Ezra Pound, Canto 74

An old poet locked up with a gang of murderers and rapists, Crazy Ez surveys the wreckage of Europe in summer 1945:

Haec sunt fastae—"here are festivals": mixed irony and mystic vision; the only festivals in the death camp existed in the poet's mind.

Under Taishan quatorze Juilet—Under Taishan 14 July—Taishan, a sacred mountain to Confucians, like the festivals, exists only in the poet's mind. 14 July—Bastille Day.

with the hill ablaze north of Taishan—Another vision that war and death-camps cannot erase.

and Amber Rives is dead, the end of that chapter
    see Time for June 25th
Amber Rives, an English novelist Ez liked and often played tennis with before World War I.

Mr Graham himself unmistably, on a horse, an ear and a beard's point showing
Cunningham Graham, novelist and pacifist, who rejected his pacifist ideals to serve in World War I.

and the Farben works still intact—I.G. Farben Werke, a major supplier to Hitler's war machine, never got hit by a single Allied bomb; "intact" as in *virgo intacta.*

I can only think of three reasons why Farben never got bombed while most of Europe was reduced to rubble:

1. American banks owned a large part of Farben.

2. American interests, already planning a war with Russia, knew they would need the Farben Werke.

3. The allied command kept aiming at Farben but due to stupidity or incompetence just kept hitting civilian populations hundreds of miles away.

You pays yr money & you takes yr cherce.

ART AS SOCIAL COMMENTARY

Wim Delvoye, a Belgian artist, has brought what he considers his latest and most important work, "Cloaca," to the New Museum of Contemporary Art in Manhattan, New York, USA. "Cloaca" duplicates the human digestive system from mouth to anus.

Twice a day, "Cloaca" is fed a healthy meal provided by one of New York's upscale restaurants, and twice a day the machine produces human shit from this food.

A computer brain monitors the introduction of bacteria, enzymes, pepsin, pancreatin, and hydrochloric acid. After six stages of digestion in jars based on human organs, much of the liquid is removed from the product and the solid shit expelled onto a revolving conveyor belt.

[Source: Michael Teters e-mail: tetersms@UMDNJ.EDU]

"It Drippeth as the Gentle Rain from Heaven"

SALT LAKE CITY, Utah—The shit definitely hit the fan and every other part of a home in Utah. A shower of dung from a reportedly unknown source covered two sides of the home, the backyard and a hot tub.

When similar blobs hit homes in Salt Lake County in spring 1999, homeowners blamed aircraft for dumping septic tanks in flight. But in this last incident, the mess was devoid of tell-tale blue chemicals used in plane's toilets, and officials from the Federal Aviation Administration maintain that aircraft do not have the ability to empty their tanks while flying.

[Source: News of the Bizarre]

Well, if Modern Art and the Paranormal Realm have the same comment on our post-TSOG world, maybe we should consider their judgment?

*Coming Soon from
New Falcon...*

THE TALE OF THE TRIBE

ALPHABET/IDEOGRAM

JOYCE/POUND

SHANNON/McLUHAN

TV/ INTERNET

a somewhat interactive exploration

by Robert Anton Wilson

ALL * STAR* CAST *OF *CHARACTERS*

What do Giordano Bruno, Giambatista Vico, **Friedrich Nietzsche**, Ernest Fenollosa, Ezra Pound, Alfred Korzybski, James Joyce, Buckminster Fuller, Claude Shannon, Marshall McLuhan and Internet all have in common?

Simple answer: they have all influenced my way of "thinking" (perceiving/conceiving the world).

A more complicated answer makes up the rest of the book...

Giordano Bruno (1548–1600), a Neapolitan trouble-maker, has strongly influenced both modern science *and* modern occultism—an oddly mixed heritage. Bruno's "pantheism" also had major philosophic impact on Spinoza; in the 20th Century he has continued to exert a fascination upon such odd bedfellows as Annie Besant, of the Theosophical Society; **Wilhelm Reich**, radical psychotherapist; **Timothy Leary**, another radical psychotherapist; and on **Joyce** and **Pound**. Paul Levinson regards Bruno's de-centered universe as the perfect model of **cyberspace.**

eh, the perfect model of cyberspace?

Bruno's books got burned by the holy roman catholic and apostolic church. They also burned Bruno himself 17 February

1600. When surrounded by barbarians, it may prove hazardous to have new ideas.

Bruno's universe, infinite in both space and time, has no "real" or absolute center, since wherever you cut a slice out of infinity, infinity remains. Thus every place an observer stands becomes a relative center for that observer.

Cyberspace, an indefinite but ever-growing network, also has no absolute center. Every console becomes "the" center for it's user.

Plug in a terminal. The net doesn't care who or what you think you "are."

...language as Class Warfare...

Giambasta Vico (1668–1744): Another tricky Neapolitan writer, so egregious and/or polymathic that one finds him called a "philosopher," a "sociologist," and even a precursor of "cultural anthropology" or "Jungian psychology." A heavy influence on Hegel and Marx; on **Joyce** and **Pound;** and on Transpersonal Linguistics. **Joyce** (and the present book) borrow most heavily, not from Vico's "cycle" theory of history, but from his concept of language as Class Warfare.

Vico, unlike Bruno, escaped the Inquisition, but frequently got himself accused of "heresy" by academic rivals; at his funeral, a violent confrontation broke out between his admirers and a group of detractors, still charging "heresy" and declaring him unfit for burial in "holy ground" (the cemetery of the University of Naples, where he had taught). Some of the disputants required hospitalization afterwards; Neapolitans take philosophy seriously.

Marx bragged of "turning Hegel upside down," thinking he had thereby created Social Science. Unfortunately, metaphysics turned upside down does not become science but merely upside-down metaphysics. Hence the failure of Marxism.

Friedrich Nietzsche (1844–1900) offbeat German philologist-philosopher, enemy of "morality"; often (inaccurately) blamed for

World War I, Nazism, World War II, Existentialism, the Leopold-Loeb murder, and other nefarious tendencies and events. Influence on Sigmund Freud, Carl Jung, Thomas Mann, W.B. Yeats, Stefan George, Bernard Shaw, Jean-Paul Sartre, Eugene O'Neill, William Faulkner and, of course, **Joyce** and **Pound**. We will consider him chiefly as a critic of language and forerunner of Wittgenstein, Logical Positivism, **Pound/Joyce** and General Semantics.

Ernest Fenollosa (1853–1908), scholar of and historian of art, Eastern and Western; considered a "national hero" in Japan, and buried as such with all due honors by the Japanese government, Fenollosa remains mostly unknown in his own country (U.S.A.) Revered in Japan for renewing interest in Japanese poetry and painting at a time when the young Japanese mostly had forgotten their own tradition and wanted to imitate Western models, Fenollosa also wrote an essay on "The Chinese Written Character as a Medium for Poetry"[10] which vastly influenced **Ezra Pound** and, through Pound, modern poetry generally; said essay also anticipates some formulations of General Semantics and Neuro-Linguistic Programming (NLP), and foreshadows modern critiques of "linear" and "alphabetical" thinking.

> A squiggly fractal—
> the line of Monterrey's hills—
> floats above the fog

...the alphabet vs. the equation...

---

10 Given to Ezra Pound, 1913, by Fenollosa's widow. After five years of Homeric struggles to get this essay published, Pound printed it as an appendix to a book of his own literary/linguistic essays, *Instigations* (1918). In 1952, *Instigations* having gone out of print, Pound, **Marshall McLuhan** and associates reprinted it as part of their Square Dollar Series. (A search of the World Wide Web 7 Feb. 2000 indicates that this revolutionary essay has again gone out of print.)

Count Alfred Korzybski (1879–1950) inventor of General Semantics; a Polish-born engineer, who grew up in a house where everybody spoke four languages (Polish, Russian, French, German), Korzybski wrote his major works in English after becoming a U.S. citizen. His basic theorems: [1] every "language" or code has a **structure** which heavily influences the perceptions and "ideas" of those who use it; [2] the *structure* of Indo-European subject-predicate sentences does not mesh with the structure of the world known to science; [3] mathematics does mesh neatly with science [4] we need to make our languages more like mathematics if we want our social life to become as pragmatically successful as our sciences. In the present context, Korzybski's mathematized language structures, like the **Fenollosa/Pound** emphasis on Chinese ideogram, helps us perceive/conceive **Internet** in alternative ways, not possible for those restricted to Indo-European semantic structures.

> "Weep, weep!" cries a bird
> Lost somewhere in fog and mist.
> Sunrise with no sun.
>
> You speak to me of nationality,
> language, religion. These are nets
> I shall try to fly over.
> — *A Portrait of the Artist as a Young Man*

James Joyce (1882–1941), the primary inventor, along with **Pound**, of "modernism" in literature. In *Dubliners* (1914), Joyce invented the "modern" (*New Yorker*-style) short story, or slice-of-life; in *A Portrait of the Artist as a Young Man* (1915), he changed the style and language continually, from infant prattle to educated elegance, as the hero grew from babyhood to college graduation; in *Ulysses*[11] (1922), he replaced the allegedly "objective" and seemingly omniscient narrator of traditional fiction with a hundred narrators (or "narrative voices") all of them mildly-to-severely

---

[11] Banned from U.S. and repeatedly burned 1922–1933. The Lying Bastards said they wanted to protect us from "indecency."

distorting events to suit their own predilections; in *Finnegans Wake* (1939) he invented a new hologrammic style, based on **Bruno** and **Vico**, which encodes the whole into every part. In this book we lean most heavily upon the neurological relativism of *Ulysses* and the hologrammic prose of *Finnegans Wake.*

> free speech without free radio speech is as zero
> — Ezra Pound, Canto 74

Ezra Pound (1885–1971)[12] a foremost creator of and *the* primary polemicist and propagandist for "modernism" in literature and art; proponent of "ideogrammic" as distinguished from "alphabetical" (linear) perception and/or conception of world; major influence on **McLuhan**.[13] I borrow mostly from Pound's use of ideogrammic method in his epic *Cantos* (1917–1970 approx.) and in *Machine Art* (1930).

> Gay flamingo sings:
> "The sun rises and the world
> Is ablaze with Dawn"

...the alphabet vs. the equation...?
...language as Class Warfare...?

R. Buckminster Fuller (1895–1983), often hailed as "the modern Leonardo," "the brainiest American since Benjamin Franklin," etc.; inventor of the Geodesic Dome, the World Game,[14] the Dymaxion Car, the Dymaxion Map (the first 2-dimensional projection to show all continents without distortion), the Global

---

[12] Charged with "treason"(poor usage of the First Amendment) by the U.S. government; committed to St. Elizabeth's Hospital for the Criminally Insane for 13 years, 1945–1958.

[13] **A WORD TO THE WISE GUY:** Quick like a bunny, check out: http://www.chass.utoronto.ca/mcluhan-studies/v1_iss1/1_1art11.htm.

[14] **A WORD TO THE WISE GUY:** Quick like a bunny, check out: http://www.worldgame.org/wwwproject/.

Energy Network, Synergetic Geometry, etc. etc. etc. inventor of the phrase "Spaceship Earth" etc. Here we mostly use Fuller's synergetic/planetary sociology, as influenced by and an influence upon **Pound.**

> God is not a noun.
> God is a verb.
> — Buckminster Fuller, No More Second-Hand God

Marshall McLuhan (1911–1980). Who he? You'll find out.

Claude Shannon (1916–) never had any trouble with the Proper Authorities, but he nonetheless launched two mathematical revolutions which made **Internet** inevitable and also crept into the vocabulary of both the biological and social sciences: In his 1940 M.S. dissertation for M.I.T. he demonstrated how use of Boolean algebra could make electrical networks into logic machines, thereby creating the theory of digital circuits, the foundation stone of modern computers; and in his 1948 book, *The Mathematical Theory of Communication* (University of Illinois Press), he created Information Theory, which underlies **Internet** and simultaneously acted as a paradigm for literally dozens of other sciences.

I actually find it hard to think of any area of modern life—science, education, business, art, entertainment—where bits and bytes of Shannon's Information Theory have *not* penetrated. In fact, whenever you tell somebody how many "bits" (binary units) a disk contains, you have quoted him... And whenever you've heard or used the word "feedback" in any but its original meaning[15], you have heard another extension of Shannon's work.

---

[15] Sound distortion created by interacting electronic systems.

"f-e-e-d-b-a-c-k..."

$$H = -\Sigma p_n \log_e p_n$$

> — Claude Shannon,
> *The Mathematical Theory of Communication*

Shit, motherfucker! I want my fucking money, motherfucker.

I'm still hungry.

> — *Citizen Kane*

You'll get fat!

> — *The Magnificent Ambersons*

Another lobster, and a New York steak...

> — *F For Fake*

and featuring in a special cameo role, *ORSON WELLES*

When I was around twelve years old, I had, like most kids, a nearly insatiable desire for narrative pleasure, for stories of almost any kind... "It was possible to experience simultaneously, in various media, 'high' and 'low' culture, Shakespeare as well as Milton Berle. I can remember clearly my attachment both to the much-maligned 'horror' comics and to 'Classics Illustrated,' both to *Space Patrol* and to *Omnibus*, both to Joseph Mankiewicz's adaptation of Shakespeare's *Julius Caesar* and to Samuel Fuller's Cold War thriller *Pickup on South Street*...

If my reading interests ranged from the Hardy Boys to Sherlock Holmes to *The Three Musketeers* to *Hamlet*, this was in part because of what I experienced at the

movies and on radio and television. 'Culture,' in my childhood, was a complex interweaving of high, middle and low... "This is where Orson Welles comes in..."
— *Orson Welles, Shakespeare and Popular Culture,* by Michael Anderegg, Columbia University Press, NY, 1999

in the world of Esperanza, Primrose and Augusta;
of fat fussy old women and of fat fussy old men.
"Sure they want war," said Bill Yeats,
"They want all the young gals fer themselves."
That lovely unconscious world,
slop over slop, and blue ribbons
— Ezra Pound, Canto 41

W.B. Yeats: 1865–1939
James Joyce: 1882–1941
Ezra Pound: 1885–1972

Pound went to London in 1909 with the specific intent of meeting Yeats, whom he considered the greatest living poet. If you want to become a great poet, he believed, find a great poet to learn from.

The Yeats-Pound synergy mutated both of them, stylistically. If you agree with Nietzsche that "the only way to improve your mind is to improve your style," then they both grew mentally as well as technically. Modern poetry oscillates between the poles of Pound and Yeats. Of the tribe of Ezra (and acknowledging it): William Carlos Williams, Allen Ginsberg, Charles Olsen, Sir Basil Bunting, Louis Zukofsky, e e cummings. Yeats's influence appears in W.H. Auden, Alan Tate, and most of T.S. Eliot (except "The Waste Land" which Eliot allowed Pound to "edit"—the end product looks suspiciously like a gloomy/neurotic/Christian prologue to Pound's exuberant/high-hearted/pagan *Cantos*).

In 1912, preparing an anthology of Imagist poetry, Pound asked Yeats if he could suggest any new poets not allied to the Imagist circle, but writing close enough to the Imagist style to deserve inclusion. Yeats mentioned a man who'd left Dublin under a cloud and had survived since then as a language teacher in Trieste: James Joyce.

Pound wrote to JJ; JJ sent him the "Chamber Music" poems and Pound picked two of them for the anthology. (He picked exactly the same two I would have picked, the one about the seabird going forth in the cold wind and the one about the Army marching and the sea-hags running on the beach waving their long green hair.)

EP wrote again to ask for more poems. Joyce said he currently worked in prose and sent along a few of the "Dubliners" stories.

These stories resembled NOTHING previous in world literature. They had no plots, no beginnings or middles or ends, JJ had INVENTED the "slice of life" which later became the *"New Yorker*-type story" and since then has become formalized and mass produced by mediocrities. The style (described by Joyce as "scrupulous meanness") fit the blocked, paralyzed,[16] bumbling denizens of an Occupied City the way good clothes fit a body.

Yeats belonged to several Irish rebel groups (which might have gotten him hanged if the Brits ever caught him). Joyce called himself an anarchist but remained politically aloof (Stirnerite). Yet Joyce, with the mask of "scrupulous meanness," showed in small everyday details the Death Trip hanging over an occupied country, and made ordinary nastiness as awful as Sartre ever made the major horrors of the Nazi occupation of France.

EP's reaction: "I can turn from good French prose to a page of Joyce without feeling my head is being stuffed with cotton." (Other English prose of the time did not please him.)

Pound devoted major energies to getting *Dubliners* published. When JJ began *Portrait of the Artist as a Young Man* with a new style (which starts out as baby-talk and grows up in quantum jumps as the Artist himself grows, from infancy to 20 years old), Pound again saw a major breakthrough in prose and worked like hell to get it serialized and then published in full. Then he found two rich

---

16 The first story concerns a priest who is both physically and symbolically paralyzed.

women who started sending Joyce monthly gifts to support him while he launched the even-more revolutionary *Ulysses*. Through all this, Pound never complained about his own poverty. He seems to have seen himself as a tough guy who took hard times easily and JJ as a sensibility so sensitive it might burn out without sufficient nourishment.

During World War I, Pound and Joyce corresponded a lot and agreed about the slaughter. Pound said it was a pity the nations involved couldn't ALL be defeated. JJ wrote a Swiftian poem denouncing warfare, the only overtly political work in his *ouvre*. Yeats expressed himself by writing poems in which humanity appears as "weasels fighting in a hole" and the Anti-Christ slouches toward Bethlehem to be born.

About the Author

For five years (1966–1971) Robert Anton Wilson was Associate Editor of Playboy. Since 1971 he has worked as Futurist, novelist, playwright, poet, lecturer and stand-up comic.

In the area of social philosophy, Wilson wrote such Futuristic projections as *Cosmic Trigger, Right Where You Are Sitting Now, Prometheus Rising* and *The New Inquisition.* These works have earned such praise as:

"one of the leading thinkers of the modern age"
(Barbara Marx Hubbard, World Future Society)

"one of the most important scientific philosophers of this century"
(Timothy Leary)

"a 21st Century Renaissance Man...funny, wise and optimistic...
the Lenny Bruce of philosophers"
(Denver Post)

Wilson's *Cosmic Trigger* was recently listed in first place among recommended books on the New Age by *Changing Times.*

In science-fiction, Wilson authored the *Schroedinger's Cat* trilogy which has been called "the most scientific of all science-fiction novels" (by *New Scientist*) and has been reprinted in England, Germany, Switzerland and Austria.

With Robert Shea, Wilson co-authored the *Illuminatus* trilogy which was called "the biggest sci-fi cult novel to come along since *Dune*" (by the *Village Voice*).

Illuminatus has been reprinted in many countries and adapted (by Ken Campbell) into a ten-hour epic drama which has been performed in Liverpool, London, Cambridge University, Amsterdam, Frankfurt, Jerusalem, Seattle and at the National Theatre of Great Britain under the patronage of Her Majesty Elizabeth II.

In 1986—only ten years after publication—*Illuminatus* won the Prometheus Award as a "classic" of science-fiction. In 1989, 13 years after publication, *Illuminatus* became the best-selling sci-fi paperback in the U.S. In 2002, it still holds 10th place among the top 100,000 sci-fi novels sold by Amazon.com.

Wilson's long series of historical novels—*The Earth Will Shake, The Widow's Son, Nature's God* and *Masks of the Illuminati* have been published and more are under contract—reinterprets history in a totally new way. Of this series, Philip K. Dick (author of *Blade Runner*) wrote, "Wilson managed to reverse every mental polarity in me, as if I had been pulled through infinity. I was astonished and delighted."

Wilson has appeared as stand-up comic at clubs in London, Dublin, New York, San Francisco and Los Angeles and regularly teaches seminars at New Age Centers such as Esalen (Big Sur), Oasis (Chicago), Interface (Boston), Open Center (New York).

Wilson's poetry has been widely published and, in 1986, he was a guest of the Norwegian government at the Oslo International Poetry Festival.

He has also starred on a Punk Rock record in collaboration with the Golden Horde (*The Chocolate Biscuit Conspiracy,* Hot Wire, Dublin) and a comedy record (*Secrets of Power,* Illuminated Records, London).

Wilson's play, *Wilhelm Reich in Hell* was performed at the Edmund Burke Theatre in Dublin in 1986; in Portland, Maine, 1989; in Long Beach, CA, 1989; in Ann Arbor 1996; in San Francisco 1999; and the play was read on WBAI (NY) in March 1989.

Wilson is featured in the video, *Borders,* which has been shown on many PBS TV stations and won the first prize in "visions of the future" at Whole Life Expo, San Francisco, 1989. Wilson edits the Futurist journal *Trajectories.*

Bob's website, www.rawilson.com is in the top two percent of the most visited sites on the World Wide Web.

maybe logic

The Lives and Ideas of
Robert Anton Wilson

The final secret of the Illuminati finally revealed. Really.

an interactive, randomized, dvd documentary
coming winter 2002 from deepleafproductions.com

OTHER BOOKS BY ROBERT ANTON WILSON

Chaos and Beyond
*Coincidance: A Head Test
*Cosmic Trigger I: The Final Secret of the Illuminati
*Cosmic Trigger II: Down to Earth
*Cosmic Trigger III: My Life After Death
Everything Is Under Control
*Ishtar Rising
Masks of the Illuminati
Natural Law, or Don't Put a Rubber on Your Willy
*Neuropolitics (with Timothy Leary and George Koopman)
PLAYBOY'S Book of Forbidden Words
*Prometheus Rising
*Quantum Psychology
*Reality Is What You Can Get Away With
Right Where You Are Sitting Now
*Sex, Drugs and Magick: A Journey Beyond Limits
*The Historical Illluminatus Chronicles
    *The Earth Will Shake
    *The Widow's Son
    *Nature's God
The Illuminati Papers
The Illuminatus trilogy (with Robert Shea)
    The Eye in the Pyramid
    The Golden Apple
    Leviathan
*The New Inquisition
The Sex Magicians
The Schroedinger's Cat trilogy
    The Universe Next Door
    The Trick Top Hat
    The Homing Pigeons
*The Tale of the Tribe
*TSOG: The Thing That Ate the Constitution
*The Walls Came Tumbling Down
*Wilhelm Reich in Hell

*Published by New Falcon Publications

FROM ROBERT ANTON WILSON

COSMIC TRIGGER I
Final Secret of the Illuminati

The book that made it all happen! Explores Sirius, Synchronicities, and Secret Societies. Wilson has been called "One of the leading thinkers of the Modern Age."

"A 21st Century Renaissance Man. ...funny, optimistic and wise..."
—The Denver Post

ISBN 1-56184-003-3

COSMIC TRIGGER II
Down to Earth

In this, the second book of the *Cosmic Trigger* trilogy, Wilson explores the incredible Illuminati-based synchronicities that have taken place since his ground-breaking masterpiece was first published.

Second Revised Edition!

"Hilarious... multi-dimensional... a laugh a paragraph."   *—The Los Angeles Times*

ISBN 1-56184-011-4

COSMIC TRIGGER III
My Life After Death

Wilson's observations about the premature announcement of his death, plus religious fanatics, secret societies, quantum physics, black magic, pompous scientists, Orson Welles, Madonna and the Vagina of Nuit.

"A SUPER-GENIUS... He has written everything I was afraid to write."
—Dr. John Lilly, psychologist

ISBN 1-56184-112-9

FROM ROBERT ANTON WILSON

PROMETHEUS RISING

Readers have been known to get angry, cry, laugh, even change their entire lives. Practical techniques to break free of one's 'reality tunnels'. A very important book, now in its *eighth* printing.

"*Prometheus Rising* is one of that rare category of modern works which intuits the next stage of human evolution... Wilson is one of the leading thinkers of the Modern age."
— Barbara Marx Hubbard

ISBN 1-56184-056-4

QUANTUM PSYCHOLOGY
How Brain Software Programs You & Your World

The book for the 21st Century. Picks up where *Prometheus Rising* left off. Some say it's materialistic, others call it scientific and still others insist it's mystical. It's all of these—and none.

Second Revised Edition!

"Here is a Genius with a Gee!"
— Brian Aldiss, *The Guardian*
"What great physicist hides behind the mask of Wilson?"
— *New Scientist*

ISBN 1-56184-071-8

FROM ROBERT ANTON WILSON

ISHTAR RISING
Why the Goddess Went to Hell and What to Expect Now That She's Returning

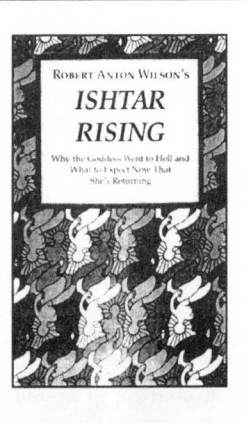

The Return of the Goddess. Wilson provides a new slant on this provocative topic. Exciting, suggestive, and truly passionate. First published by Playboy Press as *The Book of the Breast*. Updated and revised for the '90s. All new illustrations.

ISBN 1-56184-109-9

SEX, DRUGS & MAGICK
A Journey Beyond Limits

Sex, Drugs and Magick are all fascinating and dangerous subjects in these times. First published by Playboy Press, this is *the* definitive work on this important and controversial topic.

"Wilson pokes and prods our misconceptions, prejudices and ignorance."
— Ray Tuckman, *KPFK Radio*

ISBN 1-56184-001-7

THE NEW INQUISITION
Irrational Rationalism & The Citadel of Science

Wilson dares to confront *the* disease of our time which he calls 'Fundamentalist Materialism'. "I am opposing the Fundamentalism, not the Materialism. The book is deliberately shocking because I do not want its ideas to seem any less stark or startling than they are…"

ISBN 1-56184-002-5

FROM ROBERT ANTON WILSON

WILHELM REICH IN HELL

*Foreword by C. S. Hyatt, Ph.D.
and Donald Holmes, M.D.*

Inspired by the U. S. government seizure and burning of the books and papers of the world famous psychiatrist Dr. Wilhelm Reich. "No President, Academy, Court of Law, Congress, or Senate on this earth has the knowledge or power to decide what will be the knowledge of tomorrow."

"Erudite, witty and genuinely scary..."   —*Publishers Weekly*

ISBN 1-56184-108-0

COINCIDANCE

A Head Test

The spelling of the title is *not* a mistake. *Dance* through Religion for the Hell of It, The Physics of Synchronicity, James Joyce and Finnegan's Wake, The Godfather and the Goddess, The Poet as Early Warning Radar and much much more...

"Wilson managed to reverse every mental polarity in me, as if I had been pulled through infinity."
                —Philip K. Dick, author
                        of *Blade Runner*

ISBN 1-56184-004-1

New Falcon Publications

Invites You to Visit Our Website:
http://www.newfalcon.com

At the Falcon website you can:

- Browse the online catalog of all of our great titles
- Find out what's available and what's out of stock
- Get special discounts
- Order our titles through our secure online server
- Find products not available anywhere else including:
    - One of a kind and limited availability products
    - Special packages
    - Special pricing
- Get free gifts
- Join our email list for advance notice of New Releases and Special Offers
- Find out about book signings and author events
- Send email to our authors (including the elusive Dr. Christopher Hyatt!)
- Read excerpts of many of our titles
- Find links to our author's websites
- Discover links to other weird and wonderful sites
- And much, much more

Get online today at http://www.newfalcon.com